STEP BY STEP BEGINNERS GUIDE TO RAISED BED GARDENING, HARVESTING AND PRESERVING

A BEGINNERS GUIDE TO CREATING AND PRESERVING VIBRANT LUSH GARDENS

KATE GREEN

© **Copyright 2022 - All rights reserved.**

The content contained within this book may not be reproduced, duplicated or transmitted without direct written permission from the author or the publisher.

Under no circumstances will any blame or legal responsibility be held against the publisher, or author, for any damages, reparation, or monetary loss due to the information contained within this book, either directly or indirectly.

Legal Notice:

This book is copyright protected. It is only for personal use. You cannot amend, distribute, sell, use, quote or paraphrase any part, or the content within this book, without the consent of the author or publisher.

Disclaimer Notice:

Please note the information contained within this document is for educational and entertainment purposes only. All effort has been executed to present accurate, up to date, reliable, complete information. No warranties of any kind are declared or implied. Readers acknowledge that the author is not engaged in the rendering of legal, financial, medical or professional advice. The content within this book has been derived from various sources. Please consult a licensed professional before attempting any techniques outlined in this book.

By reading this document, the reader agrees that under no circumstances is the author responsible for any losses, direct or indirect, that are incurred as a result of the use of the information contained within this document, including, but not limited to, errors, omissions, or inaccuracies.

CONTENTS

Introduction   5

1. MAKING A PLAN   9
   Why Raised Beds?   10
   Preparing your Site   12

2. BUILDING RAISED BEDS   15
   Best and Worst Materials for Building Raised Garden Beds   15
   Tools, Supplies and Instructions   18
   Basic Raised Bed Plans   19

3. SOIL CARE BASICS   25
   How Does Soil Work?   26
   Soil Tips   29

4. TO GROW OR NOT TO GROW   33
   Starting Plants Inside   34
   Companion Planting   37
   Root Vegetables   38
   Greens   47
   Vining   56
   Branching/Stalks   62
   Fruit   73
   Herbs   80
   Flowers   94
   What (Maybe) Not to Grow   112
   Planning to Plant   114

5. PLANTING AND MAINTAINING … 115
    Water … 116
    Fertilizer … 119
    Troubleshooting: Pests, Mold, and
    Disease Control … 123

6. HARVEST YOUR GARDEN … 135
    When Is It Time to Harvest Your
    Vegetables? … 136
    Extend Your Harvest … 137
    After the Harvest … 138
    Plan for Next Year … 143

7. CANNING AND PRESERVING … 145
    What Is Canning? … 146
    Pickling Recipe … 152
    Salt Water … 154
    Salsas and Sauces … 154
    Syrup … 156
    Jams … 156
    Freezing … 158
    Drying Herbs … 159
    Pressing Flowers … 160
    Potpourri … 160

    Conclusion … 163
    References … 167

INTRODUCTION

Simply planting a seed is enough to see a sprout but it isn't the method that will produce the most bountiful harvests. Plants want to live—gardening isn't difficult because there are a million steps, it is difficult because the execution of the few steps make a difference. Raised garden beds accentuates gardeners abilities to provide the optimal situation for these plants to produce strong, fruitful harvests. This book introduces to beginners how to create a micro-environment developed especially for the plants needs. Even in their natural environment these plants are only about to survive. The point of raised gardens is to make them thrive.

Growing up on a farm I knew what to expect from these plants. When I ventured into gardening in my adulthood I realized that I wasn't getting such lush plants as I remembered in my childhood. One summer after tending to my garden every day I realized I hadn't noticed any watermelon growing yet. I went to investigate and found a single grape-sized melon. I kept an eye on it and it didn't get larger than a plum the whole season. This was the point where I knew that I needed to do something else.

Gardening is a passion and a pain. When you are getting started it can feel like there is too much all at once. Then you have to deal with having so much time and energy invested into these fussy plants. I wish someone had told me when I just started gardening how many plants I would kill. As a beginner it can feel crushing to see a plant go from full health to compost overnight. Raised gardening beds prevent many of the issues that cause this but sometimes a plant just dies. That doesn't mean gardening is not worth your time though, it is the most fulfilling and functional project there is.

Raised beds allowed me to stop working backwards by starting from a clean slate instead of constantly battling problems. They give an opportunity to create a small plant oasis. By focusing on advancing this small area instead of trying to tackle the entire space means you are not spreading your resources thin. You are able to maneuver through your garden easier which means being able to address issues like adding support or pesticides without trampling anything. It creates an intentional area that can be easily fenced in from rabbits and deer as well.

This book will give an in depth explanation on how to create this dream. We will start with making a plan to create optimal results by making intentional choices on location and desired plants. Then we will look at how to actually build these raised beds, what soil you will need, what plants to grow, how to plant and take care of them, how to harvest and even how to preserve your harvest. You will have all the tools to create the garden that will care for you the same way you care for it.

I want everyone to be able to successfully garden year after year. I think that it is everyone's right to be able to grow their own food organically. Gardening should be accessible to everyone. Having the same tools that I do now will allow you to skip some unnecessary learning curves. The joy that gardening gives me should be something that everyone is able to experience and the taste of home-grown food is beyond comparison to food from the grocery store. The food there is often picked before it is ready so that it will survive transportation which doesn't allow the flavors to develop as strongly. Home grown food is not a mystery either, you are able to eat it with confidence in where it has come from.

Gardening is very personal which means that every garden is going to look different. There are a million different ways to grow, but the basics to creating a healthy garden look the same. In the following chapter we will look at how to start planning this garden so that your expectations and reality can meet.

1

MAKING A PLAN

The first step of creating a successful garden is to set yourself up to succeed by making a plan. There needs to be decisions in place before you break ground. This chapter covers how to choose a site for your garden while chapter 4 goes over the best plants to consider growing. Chapter 4 should be considered when creating a plan because it will greatly affect what conditions you need to choose your location. Having an idea of which plants you are growing and how many of them you intend to plant also means that you can determine the space you need.

WHY RAISED BEDS?

Part of your garden plan should be a raised bed. While it is possible to garden directly in the ground it does not provide the plants with the same care as a raised bed. This means that before you even start there is going to be a significant disadvantage and therefore a less prosperous harvest.

The benefit of raised gardens starts at accessibility. This accessibility is twofold in that it creates access regardless of location as well as being easier to physically work on. In almost every location you can raise a raised garden bed, whether this be a tiny front garden, a community garden, or an expansive backyard. This means that even if there is no garden initially in place, a raised garden bed can be placed anywhere a plant pot can fit. In the second case of physical ability, a raised garden bed allows gardeners to maneuver easier in their gardens. When gardeners can get to their plants easier and from more angles, they are able to take care of them and assess their needs better. In addition to that, depending on the height of the garden it can mean that gardeners who have trouble kneeling, bending or other movements are able to work on their garden.

Soil is the next reason to consider a raised bed. The soil you may have in your backyard (or wherever you may be considering growing plants) is unlikely to be the most optimal for growing plants. Most of the plant's nutrients are stored in the dirt. Raised beds create a concentrated area of ideal soil so that it requires significantly less. Chapter 3 goes over soil in more detail. Because of the side panels on a raised garden bed it means that the soil is not eroded over time.

The smaller concentrated space means that you save water. Instead of spraying a larger area you only need to water the raised bed. Since it is enclosed it also means that the water isn't running off or soaking into the ground.

A combination of the smaller space and the fresh dirt means that a raised bed has less weeding. Weeds are not just visually unappealing, they suck the nutrients out of the soil and even suffocate intended plants. With fresh dirt, it means there aren't any hidden or dormant seeds for these weeds.

The last reasoning to choose a raised bed is that it means more plants per square foot. Even if you are not encumbered by space restrictions, a concentrated area of higher yield means that you are able to fit in more plants and produce a higher crop. This is especially important when it comes to growing food.

PREPARING YOUR SITE

As previously mentioned, there are a lot of factors to consider when choosing the specifics of your garden site. One of the first decisions is what size it will be. Of course the width is greatly going to be affected by the space you have to work with. The height is going to be affected by the needs of you as an individual (accessibility). Besides these factors size can be affected by the other following factors in defining your site: functionality, convenience, aesthetics.

Size and functionality go hand in hand. Depending on the kind of plants you want to grow and the amount of yield you are hoping to produce, the size of the garden bed(s) will vary. Other things you should consider about functionality is staking, sunlight, shelter, and water. If you are planning on growing plants that need support then you need to consider the spacing and placement. Chapter 2 goes over this a little more. Sunlight is another factor that is going to make a huge impact on your location choice. Depending on the plants you want to grow you might need a location that provides shelter from the harshest sunlight of the day. The strength of these plants and the local weather might mean that your raised garden would be best placed near a building or trees to add some shelter from wind and rain. On the other hand, gardens too close to a building might result in being targeted by rain water runoff. The last part of functionality to consider is whether you are going to be able to access water. The hose must be able to reach the garden and not be a hazard to you or your backyard.

Convenience is an extension of functionality. When you consider what is best for the plants, you also need to consider what is best for you. While you might be able to reach the area with your hose, also consider the amount of work that is required. This is a job that needs to be done regularly so make sure that you are making your life easy.

If you have more than one box or have it close to other things, how will you remove grass? If you are able to plan the gardens to be in a space where you don't end up with this problem you will thank yourself every time you cut your lawn. If you do end up having weeds or debris of other kinds, it is good to be able to get a wheelbarrow close to be able to remove it. When you are filling the raised gardens with soil, consider how far you will need to transport the soil and how easy you are going to be able to do that.

While you are considering yourself, remember that you are putting this garden in your space. If you are going to be looking at this fixture, then make sure that it compliments your space in a way you are happy with.

Just because it might be optimal real estate right in the middle of the lawn when it comes to sunlight doesn't mean you should sacrifice that continuity of the space. You should find a balance between functionality and fun.

In the next chapter these plans can come to life. We cover the materials to use, the tools you will need, trellises and fences. In combination with this chapter you will start to see your vision come to life.

2

BUILDING RAISED BEDS

Raised beds do not need to be expensive, but there are things that you should consider in creating the best bed for you. The following chapter covers what materials you should consider, what tools that you will need, and other specific customizations that you might need to consider.

BEST AND WORST MATERIALS FOR BUILDING RAISED GARDEN BEDS

It can be tempting to use whatever material is available. Gardening can be expensive, but that doesn't mean that all materials are safe to use. The following section goes over the materials to avoid, the materials you can use and the best options if possible.

Bad

- Chemically treated wood should be avoided at all costs. This includes materials that come from **pallets** and **railroads**. The chemicals that are used to treat this wood can seep into the soil which is then absorbed by the plants.
- **Tires** are dangerous similarly to how chemically treated wood is. Overtime chemicals from the tires can start to seep into the dirt and taint the plants causing them to be dangerous for human consumption.

Not everyone has the chance to opt for the better materials, so a way to make these materials more safe to use is to line the bed with plastic lining. This plastic lining should be made for this use because it will be strong and safe to use in your garden. If this is the case then take care when using sharp tools not to puncture the plastic. Replace it whenever possible since it is an inconvenient task, such as before adding compost in the spring if you notice it is being worn out. Plastic lining might even be a way to extend your wood's lifespan as it prevents the garden's water from leaking through. However, if you choose a plastic lining remember that it will hold water longer and it might change the watering requirements for your garden.

Metal sounds like a nice stable material to work with, but it can also seep into your soil as well as rust.

Good

Untreated wood is one of the most common ways to create a raised bed. As long as the wood is untreated it is safe to use. There are good, better and best types of lumber to use though.

What's the best wood? The best wood is typically cedar. Because it is natural, it will break down over time, but it will last longer than some of the alternatives. It is also appealing for its pleasing look.

Rock and bricks are also great building materials to use. You should be conscious of the type of rock or brick you are using because some types can also contain toxins such as heavy metals. Depending on the size and shape you might also find that you need to use a mortar to hold the wall together.

Pot and Beds

Even if you are reading this from an apartment building with no outdoor space to work with, it doesn't mean that you aren't able to consider growing your own food. Pots can function as a raised garden bed. Be conscious of the type of material that you are using, plastic is even okay as long as you look into the type of plastic and make sure that it is non-toxic for plants. Otherside make sure that no matter the material that it has drainage.

TOOLS, SUPPLIES AND INSTRUCTIONS

There are many kits available, but building your own is easy and more cost effective. When you build your own you are able to adjust the plans to your preferences. If you need your bed built quickly, if you don't have the tools or space to make your own, or if you need a long-lasting plastic or composite system that's easy to clean and move, a pre-fab kit is the better choice for your situation. Some of these kits are going to be made of the flimsiest material which might be ideal for those who just want a smaller or less permanent raised bed.

You will need a hammer, measuring tape, saw, shovel, and a staple gun.

Clear the area where you plan to have your garden. Even if you plan to use a liner for the bed, it is a good idea to hoe the ground to remove weeds, grass and rocks. In the future you might remove the lining and it will be much harder to work the ground. If you are using a liner then this will allow drainage to work optimally as well. Depending on your plan, you might want to remove the grass in the areas surrounding the gardens as well and replace it with gravel or stone. This will make it so the area doesn't become muddy and eroded with the traffic in the spring. It will also create some distance between the garden and the grass which means it will reduce the amount of weeding.

You might choose the option of using poles at each corner to create support. This is a good idea for all gardens but more important if your beds are taller. If you are building your raised beds just slightly off the ground you might not need to support the poles, and the side panels will be enough to keep the soil in. The taller the garden gets, the more important it is to have poles with your raised bed, the poles in the ground keep it from tipping over or bursting at the seams.

Walk around the space you have planned out. It can be really inconvenient to change your plans when you've started but you might run into a problem that you didn't predict. For instance maybe you thought there was enough space to kneel between the garden and the fence but realize that you need another few inches.

Before planting take note of how the sun hits it all day.

BASIC RAISED BED PLANS

When you are choosing the size of your garden, consider how you are going to be planting as well as working with the space you are in. If you plan on planting things like potatoes that do best in rows, you will want to make your dimensions longer to allow decent rows. Also consider how far you can reach and access the center of the garden. A garden about 4 feet wide will allow you access across.

For a basic raised bed, your four pieces of lumber should be 2x10 planks. Unless your garden will be perfectly square, you will need to cut two of the planks for the longer sides, and two planks for the shorter size. If you are using poles in each corner you can make your cuts a perfect flat 180 degrees. If you are going to nail the planks together at the corners you will need to cut them on a 45 degree angle so they fit into each other.

If you are using a pole, cut the four poles to the same length. Use a measuring tape and mark the corners of the garden. Be very precise. Dig a hole deep enough so that the poles are stable, about 1 foot. Put the poles in and fill the dirt back in, making sure the poles are straight. Use a drill to screw in nails (2 ½ inch deck nails) in the corners to fasten the planks to the poles or each other. Repeat each side.

If you are going to use a liner for your bed, lay it out now. Then fill with soil. Now your garden is ready for planting.

Prepare for Climbing Plants

A trellis is a support system for plants that climb or tend to fall over. There are a huge variety of trellises because each plant grows in a different way. This isn't something that you should think about after you build your garden. A trellis can create a wall of plants that can block out the plants behind it, take up a lot of space, not be ideal for the type of plant, be harder to access in rows and so on.

Depending on the plant it might need to grow upwards, but if it is light like morning glories a string would be enough support. On the other hand, tomatoes don't need something to climb on but they become very top heavy, especially when the fruit is being produced and it will need to be held up by something sturdy enough. It's really important that produce is off the ground as much as possible. This will cause it to rot quicker and allow bugs easier access.

A-frame trellis is two panels that lean onto each other to make an A shape. The benefit of these is that it angles the plant so it can be easier to access and better for growing. The space in the center might work to your benefit so that the often chaotic vining plants are spread out a bit, but it can also be a waste of space if you aren't able to plant anything underneath due to sunlight or accessibility.

Wire trellis is a single panel of wire in whatever desirable pattern or spacing you determine. It typically is held up by stakes in the ground. Unless reinforced, a wire trellis might be less stable. It takes up less space than an A-frame trellis and can provide access to both sides of the panel. A wire trellis might also look like a wire cage. These cages are used to support plants that end up top heavy and leaning over. As long as the wire support is short enough it can provide a strong support.

Arch trellis is similar to an A-frame but much bigger. An arch typically is big enough to walk through. The benefits of this is that it leaves a lot of room to plant below it. This can even work in your favor if you want to provide shape to some plants. The downside is that it can be harder to access if its overtop of other growth and because of the height of harvest on the top.

String trellis is made from two poles a distance apart and layers of string wrapped between them. This is a more spacious option and can be done by hand for free. It does not provide as much support as wire would but is more flexible. This will need to be redone every year. This is ideal for lighter plants or plants that need more guidance than support. For example, green beans can use string support on either side to prop themselves up, because while they don't vine, they can become top heavy as they get taller. String is often enough to keep them up.

Ladder trellis is similar to a wire trellis in that it is a flat vertical panel. It is made of wood, and classically would be narrow with horizontal runs like a ladder. This has been adapted to be closer to a lattice. Like the wire trellis it takes up less room, but without reinforcement it can be unstable. Wood also deteriorates over time. A ladder trellis might be more appealing to plants like squash that are much larger. A ladder trellis is often wider than wire and has space for the large produce to lean on.

Fences

Fences are a detail that are up to the gardener. Depending on the area they might not see a need. A fence already around the back yard might be enough for some. For others they might need to fence in the area. A thin wire fence can be enough to keep rabbits out, but if your issues are birds or squirrels there might need to be more action taken. This might take shape in a roof enclosure or individual plant cages.

It might not seem ideal to have to put a fence in, but once you start off with a great garden and you are doing everything right, nothing is worse by having it ruined by things out of your control like pests big or small.

In the following chapter we will go over soil, what it holds, what it needs, and store bought versus compost.

3

SOIL CARE BASICS

It may seem dumb as dirt to spend so much talking about it, but soil is going to have a huge impact on your plants ability to thrive. Soil has two main features that need to be considered, its drainability and the nutrients that it holds. Most people know that under or over watering is a big determiner on your plants success, but it's the soil that holds the plant that is going to determine if the water is being held to the roots for long or if it is going to drain away. The soil's ability to drain also affects how long the nutrients are going to stay in the soil, because as the water is being washed away, so are the nutrients. On plants that grow taller, having soil that has some hold can also affect its ability to support the soil. If the soil is too dense it may affect the plants ability to root deeply. The following chapter goes over all the specifics on soil and how to choose the best one for your needs.

HOW DOES SOIL WORK?

The soil holds the nutrients the plants need to survive and grow. The substances that plants need are **nitrogen, oxygen, carbon, phosphorus, and potassium**. The secondary minerals that they need are **calcium, sulfur, and magnesium**. Some plants need more or less of these things, and some even add these things back into the soil. This is important to know when choosing or creating your soil. Chapter 5 goes deeper into figuring out how to supplement these nutrients and minerals with fertilizer, which includes manure and compost.

Best Soil Mixes for Raised Beds

There are two options when it comes to getting soil, you are either going to purchase it or make it yourself. If you're purchasing bags of soil, it becomes more complicated than just bags of dirt. Depending on your area you might also be able to source dirt/compost/manture by the truckload instead of by bags. This might not be something that is ideal for everyone but it can be cheaper and more accessible for some.

Types of Dirt

All purpose potting mix: As the name implies, All purpose potting mix is made with the intention of general potted plants. The pots are often sterilized which is ideal for dirt inside the home so that there are no germs to kill your indoor plants. It is a mix of peat moss, perlite, and vermiculite. Similarly is **succulent mix** which is meant to drain quickly so it doesn't cause root rot to the succulents. It's partly potting mix but it has sand, small stones, grit, and the like mixed in.

Top soil or black soil/earth: Top soil is intended for outside as the top layer of ground which is composed of organic material and a variety of different soil types. It is used as a general purpose soil and not specifically used for gardening. It can improve drainage. Lower grade might be used for filling ground, higher grade might be used for improving overall soil quality but it isn't ideal for gardening. Similar is **lawn soil** which is not as thin as top soil. The dirt is more dense with rocks. This soil is ideal for grass so that it holds on to water a bit better and the rocks allow it to breath, but not ideal for gardening.

Garden mix/triple mix: Triple mix is a mix of peat moss, top soil and compost and it is a type of gardening soil. Garden mix is a variety of different mixes.

Compost: Compost is organic matter that has decomposed into soil. Compost is very strong or concentrated and isn't meant to be used on its own. It is a great way to enhance the current soil.

Manure: Manure is animal poop. Sheep is considered the best, but other animals can be used as well but sometimes more for filling instead of enhancing or replenishing nutrients. Manure is meant to be mixed in with current soil.

Raised bed soil: When it comes to filling the raised bed there is actually a mix that is preferred specially for the raised bed instead of the gardening soil. It is nutrient rich and has good drainage.

Making Your Own Compost

Making your own compost is a great way to save money, and can be done pretty much anywhere. Your location is going to determine how much you are going to be able to do, but either way it's a good way to reuse your scraps instead of wasting nutrient-filled skins and cores. You might use a compost bin outside, but there are also table-top composters for those with less space.

Making your own compost does require some consideration. Depending on what you put in your compost you are going to affect what nutrients are in there. Coffee grounds are a common addition to compost but they are extremely acidic. If your ground has a high pH, meaning its more basic, then this might be a way to balance your garden, but if you have high acidity then this is only going to make it worse. In Chapter 6 when discussing fertilizers, we expand more on soil pH and how to balance it.

You should turn, or mix your compost but not too often. Give it at least six weeks to start breaking down on its own. Then use a shovel or gardening fork to turn the soil over. This helps quicken the composting process. Don't do it too often though because it can disrupt the little ecosystem growing too much to start working.

SOIL TIPS

Raised garden bed soil does not have to be deep: When this kind of high quality raised bed soil mix is created, it doesn't need to be spread thick. This nourishing fertile mixture will support various plants even if it is only 6 inches deep. Be sure to line the bottom of the raised bed with thick layers of cardboard (sheet mulching), newspaper, or landscaping fabric. The lining helps prevent plant roots from contacting native soil and prevent weeds from growing up into the rich soil. Just make sure that the plants that you intend to plant are going to be able to have deep root growth.

Soil Additives

Shredded bark, wood chips and/or sawdust break down slowly and help improve the structure of your soil. They retain water longer.

Tea grounds and composted coffee grinds provide the NPK (nitrogen, phosphorus, potassium) components. They make excellent additions to the compost heap. AVOID adding any tea bags.

Seaweed provides a good balance of nitrogen, potassium, and calcium. Seaweed is rich in potassium.

Alfalfa meal is an excellent source of nitrogen. It also provides some micronutrients, potassium, and phosphorus.

Sulfur helps increase your soil's acidity. It makes it easier for your plants to absorb calcium from the soil.

Dolomite lime helps increase the alkalinity of the soil. It also adds a good dose of magnesium and calcium.

Aged manure (a least six months) provides a wealth of minerals and nitrogen.

Wood ash in garden soils decreases the soil's acidity. Ash adds various nutrients, including potassium.

Use **perlite** instead of vermiculite because perlite holds moisture better.

Green sand releases micronutrients and potassium in a slow-release fashion.

Rock phosphate slowly releases micronutrients and phosphorus.

Bone meal provides some nitrogen and a good dose of phosphorus.

Gypsum is an excellent addition to make a well-drained soil.

Soybean meal releases nitrogen slowly and steadily.

Epsom salts provide a nice dose of sulfur and magnesium. About 1 cup per 100 feet. Epsom salts are not the same as table salt. In fact, cooking salt can be really hard on your plants and if you are putting cooked meals into your compost be conscious of how much salt you might be adding.

Blood meal provides a healthy dose of nitrogen.

Crushed up eggshells hold a lot of calcium which tomatoes especially appreciate.

Add **coffee grounds to hydrangeas** to turn their pink or white flowers blue.

Things to Avoid

Be cautious with ash. Wood ash in small amounts can be good for your compost, but coal ash, and any ash that might contain any other substance besides wood is bad. Ash is very acidic so too much can kill plants.

AVOID onion or citrus fruits. They can break down some of the beneficial nutrients in your compost.

AVOID meat and dairy in your compost.

AVOID pet waste.

AVOID weeds. While leaves and grass cuttings can add great organic matter, adding pulled weeds might spread the weeds into your garden.

If you are using **mushroom spores** to help your compost, it is recommended that you mix it with gardening soil before adding it to your garden because the compost can end up too strong on your seedlings.

Worms can be added. They will probably find their way in there anyway, but if you find your compost isn't breaking down as quickly some earthworms can help the process.

Now that we have built the foundation, the following chapter goes over what plants are the best for raised garden beds.

4

TO GROW OR NOT TO GROW

What you want to grow in your garden is your business but this chapter takes a look at some of the common plants for raised beds. This chapter might just be an inspiration list for some, but it also covers the growing requirements for the popular plants. It is divided into subsections to sort out all the many types so that it is easier to get an idea of what your garden will look like. Most importantly the second half of the chapter goes over the way to choose plants to make sure you get the optimal result. This includes what to grow and not grow together, plants that are better in other kinds of gardens, and other exceptions. These are things that are important to consider when you are in your planning stage. The raised garden bed is made to make the optimal living conditions for these plants, and the plants you put together make a huge difference on these conditions from the amount of shade and space, to the nutrients they take and put back into the soil.

STARTING PLANTS INSIDE

Some sources and even seed packs will mention or encourage starting seeds inside. This is left up to choice, some people swear by it and some people never do. There are benefits to starting inside, and some plants that do better when done so, however that is not always the case and it can create a lot more work that way. The benefits start with your location, if you live farther north you have a shorter growing season. This often leads to plants not finishing their cycle before the frost comes. Starting the plants inside can give a few weeks buffer time beforehand so that they will finish sooner in the year. If you start your seeds inside you are probably starting with a potting mix which is sterilized. This can give your seedlings a stronger start which might be necessary for some plants that are more susceptible to diseases. You can also baby these seedlings while they are in their weakest state some other ways too but providing optimal heat, sun and water. Lastly, you might be in less of a rush to plant these seedlings after the last frost. By not rushing to plant you might avoid a last surprise frost or even snow.

This might seem like an ideal setup, and it's not only appealing for the benefits, but also for the ambitious gardener who can't wait but to start their plants. However, it might not always be the best option. The number one reason is it causes more trauma to the plant to be moved around, especially when it's being ripped out of its pot. Some plants are more sensitive to this than others like plants with shallow root systems. They also need to be planted at the right depth. You might not have enough light inside. It can be hard even with a grow light to provide the light these seedlings require and they can die or become really long and lanky as they reach for the light and therefore weaker. It is really hard to get water right. Too much water will cause mold, which often happens in those store bought greenhouses. Or you might not water them enough which is likely as well since seedlings like a lot of water. If you're babying your seeds you might be less likely to thin them out by removing overcrowded weaker seedlings when they need to. Nature does all of these things a little more naturally. Lastly, the seedlings might become a little spoiled, and bringing them outside might cause them temperature shock.

Starting your seeds inside is completely up to you, and there are many good reasons on either side. If you are planning on doing this, you will want to use containers that have drainage holes. Some people save up their used containers all year for this. It is up to you whether you are comfortable using plastic for your seedlings or not. Use a drill to add drainage if you want.

Another common material used is egg cartons. For the first week or two you might want to cover the seedlings with a plastic bag or cover as they germinate. This will keep them wet so the plant can break through the seed. Spray whenever you think it needs more water. When they are an inch or so you can remove the greenhouse and introduce them to enough sunlight. Keep away from drafty windows.

The other option is that some plants are not very good at home germination. Many of the plants in this chapter refer to store bought seedlings instead. These are plants that you probably can try to grow from seed if it is your goal to try, however it is often cheaper and easier to buy the seedlings. When buying seedlings from the store make sure that they are healthy. If they are small and weak they might not make it to maturity and stay stunted.

COMPANION PLANTING

Companion planting has been done by indiginous people in the Americas for hundreds of years. The popular version of this is a mixture of corn, squash and beans. The idea is that the corn grows tall and is able to support the bean plants, the beans add nitrogen to the soil, and the squash shades the soil to retain enough moisture and prevent pests. This relationship is more beneficial to the plants than independent growing and that is the idea of this section. These plants aren't growing in a vacuum and their surrounding plants can positively or negatively affect them.

In the following section of this chapter, each plant will touch upon whether they have companion plants or plants to avoid with them. Depending on your garden some of these might work better or worse. For example if you have a raised bed that is 3 or 4 feet tall you might not find something tall like corn works in that bed because you won't be able to reach it. In these cases you might want to have these planted in a shorter raised bed intended for tall plants if accessibility is an issue.

The section is sorted by types of vegetables (root, vining, branching), fruit, herbs, and flowers. Under each plant you will find the different variations of these plants, what their ideal growth conditions are, how fast they grow (when they will be ready to harvest), any benefits or negatives, as well as ideal growing companions if they have any.

ROOT VEGETABLES

Consider that for root vegetables they need to be able to stretch out in the dirt.

✿ Carrots

Variations: There are over 40 carrot variations, and come in orange, purple, red, yellow, and white. Purple varieties tend to have more antioxidants, orange and red tend to be sweeter, paler white and yellow carrots can aid in absorbing nutrients. The main four categories for carrots are nates (long, round, and smooth with a blunt end), danvers (pointed, long, and round), chantenay (short and thick), and imperator (very long and thin). The longer the carrot variety the looser the soil needs to be.

Growing Requirements

- Sun: Full sun, might tolerate partial shade
- Soil: Loose, well-drained, sandy, high potassium
- Water: High moisture improves flavor, 1 inch a week

Sowing: Plant small brown seeds shallow, about ¼ of an inch deep. One seed per hole for newer seeds, double up if they are older. Plant at least 2–4 inches apart. Keep soil damp for the germination period.

Growth Rate: About 3–4 months.

Harvest: Pull out of the ground by the base of the stem after the recommended 3–4 months, too soon the carrot will be small, too long it will become woody.

Yield: One plant equals one carrot.

Pros: High in nutrients. Overall easy plant to grow.

Cons: Hard to evaluate underground. Can be sensitive to improper conditions, especially soil. Can be targeted by carrot weevils and carrot rust fly as well as other common pests.

Companion Plants: ✓ Grows well by lettuce, cabbage, onions, sage, and rosemary. ✗ Avoid other root vegetables as well as parsnip, fennel, and dill.

Tips: Prevent overcrowding when possible. It is encouraging to see lots of plants but long term can lose more by competition then by thinning.

✿ *Potato*

Variations: Over 4,000 potato variations. Potatoes range in size from being only a round 1 inch, to a long

6 inch. Size is not the only variation in potatoes, the texture and taste also varies. The seven categories of potatoes are russet (medium large, light brown skin, white flesh, dense), yellow (lumpy round and medium size, golden skin, yellow flesh, moist and smooth), white (small to medium, round to oblong, light brown skin, white flesh, mixed starchy and creamy), purple (medium and long, dark purple skin and flesh, firm), red (small round, smooth red skin, white flesh, moist and smooth), baby or petite (smaller versions of listed potatoes, stronger flavor), and fingerling (longer versions of listed potatoes, firmer).

Growing Requirements

- Sun: Full direct sun for *at least* 6 hours per day
- Soil: Loose, well-drained, loose, acidic, less fertile, lower nitrogen, higher phosphorus
- Water: 1–2 inches a week

Growth Rate: 3–4 months

Harvest: With a garden fork that is smaller in diameter than your potato variety, you can use the fork to dig out the potato root (or hand pull and siphon through the dirt for potatoes).

Sowing: Plant a whole or cut potato about 3 feet apart from each other. They are best grown in large rows with substantial trenches. Cover with 5 inches of dirt. If you are cutting the potato, make sure that the piece has an eye where it will grow. Eyes are little dimples or nubs growing off the potato. The eyes should be facing up.

Yield: One plant equals about 10 potatoes.

Pros: High yield, dense in nutrients. A starch with higher calories is a great addition to a garden since many vegetables are so low in calories.

Cons: Hard to evaluate underground. Does not play well with others. Takes up alot of space

Companion Plants: ✓ Grows well near plants with shallow roots including greens like lettuce, cabbage, and so on. ✗ Avoid growing near other root vegetables and vining plants that will compete for nutrients as well as tomatoes, eggplants, and fennel. Also avoid fruits because they are more likely to spread blight.

Tips: Potatoes do well in raised beds even if they don't grow well with other plants. Pinch off flowers to extend the plant's life and growth period.

✿ *Turnips and Rutabagas*

Variations: Over 30 turnip variations. The rutabaga is thought to be a cross between a turnip and a cabbage. One of the advantages for turnips is that both their roots and their leaves are edible. There are turnip varieties that have been created for a speedier harvest. Most turnip varieties are white fleshed with a pop of red skin, some with purple tops, and some that produce more greens if that is what you are looking for.

Growing Requirements

- Sun: Full sun
- Soil: Loose, well-drained, very fertile soil
- Water: Enough moisture improves flavor and texture, 1 inch a week

Sowing: Plant small round light brown seeds directly in the ground. Plant ½ deep, 1 inch apart, in large rows. Stagger planting for staggered harvest. Water deeply after sowing with a soft stream.

Growth Rate: About 1 month.

Harvest: Dust the soil off the top of the root to check for size so that it is at least 1 inch wide. Grab the base of the stems and gently pull the radish from the ground. Shake off any excess dirt.

Yield: One plant equals one turnip.

Pros: Root and greens are edible. Quick harvest time. Used as cover crop, to decompose and replenish soil. High in nutrients. They can be a natural pest repellent.

Cons: Hard to evaluate underground. Can be sensitive to too much or too little water.

Companion Plants: ✓ Repels pests, most leafy green plants, and branching plants benefit from this. Grows well with beans and peas, turnips add ground support while peas add nitrogen. Plant near aromatic herbs to repel larger animals ✗ Avoid other root vegetables such as potatoes and beets because of competition.

Tips: Turnips are not a huge fan of the heat, so early and late harvests are optimal.

✿ Beets

Variations: There are at least 20 types of beet variations. The classic beet is dark red, however they come in white, yellow and orange as well. Variations like the sugar beet are not grown in home gardens. Typical red beets are quite diverse, and when stored long become softer but more sweet. Golden is more mild in flavor. Striped beets are used for their interesting appearance in salads. Some varieties grow faster or have more greens.

Growing Requirements

- Sun: Full sun, but might tolerate a light shade
- Soil: Loose, well-drained, fertile soil

- Water: Enough moisture improves flavor and texture, 1–2 inch a week. Water when the soil looks dry

Sowing: Plant small brown seeds directly in the ground. Plant ½ deep, 1 inch apart, in large rows. Water deeply after sowing with a soft stream.

Growth Rate: About 1 ½ to 2 months.

Harvest: Dust the soil off the top of the root to check for size so that it is a good size. Grab the base of the stems and gently pull the beet from the ground. Shake off any excess dirt.

Yield: One plant equals one beet.

Pros: Root and greens are edible. Quick harvest time. Very high in many nutrients. Ground cover. Can repel damaging insects.

Cons: Hard to evaluate underground. Can be fussy without proper conditions.

Companion Plants: ✓ Grows well with leafy green plants. ✗ Avoid other root vegetables such as potatoes and turnips because of competition.

Tips: Like turnips, beets prefer cooler temperatures, so early and late harvests are optimal.

✿ Sweet Potatoes

Variations: While the vegetable of a potato and a sweet potato are similar, they are not actually related and the plant that grows them are quite different. Sweet potatoes, also known as yams, have their own varieties, ranging in color and size. Sweet potatoes are typically more dense, larger, and much sweeter than regular potatoes. While sweet potatoes are grown underground and are a root vegetable, their foliage is more vine-like. They are not necessarily climbers, but like to spread.

Growing Requirements

- Sun: Full sun
- Soil: Loose, well-drained, sandy, not particularly picky
- Water: They don't need much water. On hot days water more because they don't like the heat. Top up water if soil is very dry, otherwise about once a week

Sowing: Since the plant takes so long to reach maturity, you need to plant your sweet potatoes early enough in the year. They are planted the same as potatoes, by planting a cut potato slip about 3 feet apart from each other. Best grown in large rows with substantial trenches. Cover with 5 inches of dirt. If you are cutting the potato, make sure that the piece has an eye where it will grow. Eyes are little dimples or nubs growing off the potato. The eyes should be facing up.

Growth Rate: About 3–5 ½ months.

Harvest: Since sweet potatoes produce a larger fruit and smaller yield, in a small garden you won't need to use a fork to collect the roots. Pull the vine when it is time and reach your hand into the soil to make sure you've got all of them.

Yield: Two to four sweet potatoes per plant.

Pros: Very high in many nutrients.

Cons: Hard to evaluate underground. The large roots and expanding vines can take up a lot of room in the garden. They have a long growth rate.

Companion Plants: ✓ Grows well with garlic and other similar smell/tasting plants like onion, chives, as well as marigolds. Grows well with some leafy greens. ✗ Avoid other root vegetables and other vines due to competition. Avoid tomatoes and sunflowers because they carry more diseases sweet potatoes are susceptible to.

Tips: Make sure they are planted deep enough. Don't be shy to prune the vines.

GREENS

✿ *Lettuce*

Variations: There are many types of lettuce from iceberg, to romaine, loose leaf, and so on. Lettuce usually comes in green, but there are varieties that range from red to purple as well. The varieties of lettuce impact the texture and flavor of the leaf, for example iceberg lettuce is much more crunchy and the leaves are light green and tightly packed. Butterhead lettuce is more sweet with small round leaves. Romaine has a crunchy stem but looser leaves that are green and more bitter. Loose leaf lettuce has the most diversity in color and shape, with a milder flavor, and doesn't grow as a packed head like the others.

Growing Requirements

- Sun: Full sun, however the leaves can wilt under very hot days and require much more water
- Soil: Loose, well-drained, cool
- Water: Don't over water due to the more delicate foliage, but about two times a week, unless the weather is very hot where you may need to water more often

Sowing: Plant small tan seeds directly in the ground. Plant ½ inch deep. Start with planting more seedlings and thin out as they grow into about 4 inches in between. Rows create better access and allow airflow.

Growth Rate: From 2 months to 3 ½ months.

Harvest: For loose leaf variations you can snip off leaves as you need them. For dense heads you will need to wait until the head is ready. Do not wait too long or the plant will start to flower and go to seed. If you are regularly trimming lettuce it will keep growing back.

Yield: One plant equals 1 head of lettuce (unless you are regularly trimming loose leaf varieties).

Pros: Diverse in flavor and texture. Easy to grow. With short growing time, you can plant two or even three harvest of lettuce a year.

Cons: Can be fussy with sun and water. Attracts animals.

Companion Plants: ✓ Grows well with root and branching plants. It likes garlic, onion, and other aromatic plants. ✗ Other leafy greens like cabbage, and also broccoli and brussel sprouts. Too many vines might keep in too much moisture and attract slugs.

Tips: Try different varieties of lettuce. It can provide a large harvest, and you might crave some diversity after a while. Lettuce can not be preserved like other plants, so eat it while you can.

✿ Kale

Variations: Kale has three main varieties: curly, black, and red. Curly kale has green leaves that are wavy or curly, black kale is dark green and flat, red kale is also wavy but with red hues on the stems. Kale is thicker than lettuce and can be more bitter.

Growing Requirements

- Sun: Full Sun, tolerates partial shade, at least 6 hours
- Soil: Loose, well-drained, very fertile
- Water: Likes a lot of water, if not constant moisture

Sowing: Plant small brown seeds directly in the ground. Plant ½ inch deep. Start with planting more seedlings and thin out as they grow into about 4 inches in between.

Growth Rate: From 2- 2 1/2 months.

Harvest: . If you are regularly trimming kale it will keep growing back. Cut up to ⅓ of the outer leaves. Use sharp clean scissors. Do not wait too long or the plant will start to flower and go to seed.

Yield: One plant equals 1 head of kale unless you are regularly trimming.

Pros: Easy to grow. With short growing time, you can plant two or even three harvests of kale a year. More dense and hearty than lettuce.

Cons: Can be fussy by not having enough water. Can not be preserved.

Companion Plants: ✓ Grows well with root and branching plants and some leafy greens like spinach. It likes garlic, onion, and other aromatic plants. ✗ Other leafy greens like cabbage, and also broccoli and brussel sprouts. Partly because of competition, partly because they have the same weaknesses. If they are planted too close then any issue will affect the entire crop.

Tips: Kale can be frozen unlike lettuce and be used in smoothies.

✿ Spinach

Variations: There are different kinds of spinach. These varieties are split into three main types, savory, semi-savory and flat or smooth leaf. Smooth leaf is best for freezing, but semi-savory is favored because it is more pest resistant and savory is favored for its flavor. Rows create better access and allow airflow.

Growing Requirements

- Sun: Full sun, tolerates partial shade, at least 6 hours
- Soil: Loose, well-drained, cool
- Water: Likes a lot of small watering instead one one deep watering

Sowing: Plant small tan seeds directly in the ground. Plant ½ inch deep. Start with planting more seedlings and thin out as they grow with about 4 inches in between.

Growth Rate: From a month and a half to two months.

Harvest: If you are regularly trimming leaves it will keep growing back. Cut up to ⅓ of the plant. Use sharp clean scissors. Otherwise plant more seeds every time you harvest for continuous spinach.

Yield: One plant equals 1 bunch of spinach unless you are regularly trimming.

Pros: Easy to grow. With short growing time, you can plant many harvests of spinach a year. Can be boiled or eaten raw.

Cons: Can be fussy with heat because it likes cooler weather. Smaller plants yield smaller yields.

Companion Plants: ✓ Grows well with root and branching plants and some leafy greens like kale. It likes garlic, onion, and other aromatic plants. Grows really well with beans, peas, and marigolds. ✗ Does not like potatoes or squash. Like lettuce, too much ground cover can attract mold and slugs for spinach's more delicate leaves.

Tips: Like kale, spinach can be frozen and be used in smoothies. Can die off in the heat so if you are doing a summer harvest you might plant in partial shade. Does not like too much fertilizer.

❀ *Arugula*

Variations: Arugula is also known as rocket or garden rocket. It is favored for its peppery flavor. Arugula Coltivata (fast growing), Arugula Ortolani (strong flavor), Arugula Selvatica (wild), Olive Leaf arugula (strong flavor, smooth leaf).

Growing Requirements

- Sun: Full sun, tolerates partial shade, at least 6 hours
- Soil: Loose, well-drained, very fertile
- Water: Likes a lot of small watering instead one one deep watering

Sowing: Plant small tan seeds directly in the ground. Plant ½ inch deep. Start with planting more seedlings and thin out as they grow into about 4 inches in between. Rows create better access and allow airflow.

Growth Rate: From a month and a half to two months.

Harvest: If you are regularly trimming arugula, it will keep growing back. Cut up to ⅓ of the plant. Use sharp clean scissors. Otherwise plant more seeds every time you harvest for continuous arugula.

Yield: One plant equals 1 bunch of arugula unless you are regularly trimming.

Pros: Easy to grow. With short growing time, you can plant many harvests of arugula a year. Desirable flavor.

Cons: Can be fussy with heat because it likes cooler weather. Smaller plants yield smaller yields.

Companion Plants: ✓ Grows well with root and branching plants, especially beets and some leafy greens like lettuce. It likes garlic, onion, and other aromatic plants. ✗ Does not like any of the nightshade family which includes potatoes and tomatoes.

Tips: Like spinach it can die off in the heat so if you are doing a summer harvest you might plant in partial shade. Does not like too much fertilizer.

✿ Swiss Chard

Variations: Also known as simply 'chard,' swiss chard has many variations. Ranging in color, size, and flavor, swiss chard has a stem like celery and a leaf more comparable to kale. The stem is the part that ranges in color and makes it such a favorite in cooking from dark red to light red, to yellow, green, orange, white, and pink. The variation names typically give indication to their color like peppermint that goes from a raspberry to a white, or fordhook giant which indicates size. Some variations like red magic also have dark red foliage as well as stems. Some varieties grow faster than others.

Growing Requirements

- Sun: Full sun, might tolerate partial shade
- Soil: Loose, well-drained, very fertile
- Water: Prefers constant water over intervalled deep waterings

Sowing: Plant small brown seeds shallow two weeks before last frost, about ½ of an inch deep. Plant at least 4 inches apart. Keep soil damp for the germination period. Try planting in rows 15 inches apart. Rows create better access and allow airflow.

Growth Rate: Varieties range 1–2 ½ months.

Harvest: If you are regularly trimming chard it will keep growing back. Cut up to ⅓ of the plant. Use sharp clean scissors.

Yield: One plant equals head of swiss chard unless you have regular trimmings.

Pros: Absolute showstopper in cooking with its amazing colors. Provides a celery like stem and lettuce like leaf. High in nutrients. Can be eaten raw and cooked.

Cons: It might not do as well in heat even with proper care so you might only get one harvest out of it before the summer heat truly kicks in.

Companion Plants: ✓ Grows well by lettuce, cabbage, tomatoes, and beans. ✗ Avoid potatoes, corn, melon, squash due to competing needs.

Tips: Prevent overcrowding when possible. It is encouraging to see lots of plants but long term can lose more by competition then by thinning. Even when pruning make sure there is space for airflow to prevent pests and disease.

VINING

✿ Cucumber

Variations: Unlike many of the other plants and their variations, the variations of cucumber are really important to pay attention to. Cucumbers are the most likely plant to be pickled, and so if you are intending on making pickles you need to get the right variation for your recipe. There are over 100 types of cucumbers. The english cucumber is what you typically see in the store, it is long and thin with minor wrinkles, it is also very sweet. Other similar variations include: Tyria, American cucumbers, lemon, Persian, and so on. Pickling cucumbers might include: Northern pickling cucumber, garden, gherkins, and so on. Variations also affect flavor, crunchiness, seed, and growth rate.

Growing Requirements

- Sun: Full sun, might tolerate partial shade
- Soil: Well-drained, very fertile, warm
- Water: 1 inch a week, however might be fussy in heat and should be watered accordingly, especially when the leaves start to wilt. Letting it dry out too often can make the fruit more bitter

Sowing: Plant small large white seeds in the ground in late spring after the ground has warmed enough OR germinate inside a few weeks before. Plant 2 inches apart and thin to 9 inches when plants are established.

Growth Rate: 1 ½ months to 2 ½ months.

Harvest: Knowing your variety will help you determine when they are ready depending on how long they are. Twist or cut the cucumber off the vine when it's ready.

Yield: One plant might create 1–50 cucumbers depending on variation, conditions and luck.

Pros: High yield. Very easy to preserve. Easy to grow.

Cons: Cross pollination with other plants might not even be noticed until the fruit is cut open and reveals an inedible hybrid. Waiting time for ideal harvests increases the risk of looking at the fruit.

Companion Plants: ✓ Grows well with most plants, from greens, to branching plants, and root vegetables. It loves sunflowers. Nasturtium improves flavor. ✗ Avoid all other vining plants ESPECIALLY squash and melons. Also avoid potatoes and sage.

Tips: When they get bigger they will need support to climb up. Some think this is to help the amount of space because the plant will spread in the garden drastically, but it's actually to keep the fruit from the ground.

This will allow your cucumbers to get to a full size before you pick them. Otherwise they are more likely to get damaged, diseased, become a target of pests, or start rotting.

✿ Squash/Pumpkins/Zucchini

Variations: Pumpkins and zucchini are actually a type of squash. Some varieties of squash like gourds are grown in gardens for their ornamental value, even if they are not edible. The different variations of squash have a huge impact on fruit that is produced as you can tell from the difference between a pumpkin and a zucchini. Classic 'squash' can also range from spaghetti, butternut, acorn, garden, and so on.

Growing Requirements

- Sun: Full sun
- Soil: Very fertile
- Water: High moisture, large fruit needs lots of water

Sowing: Plant the seeds at least 1 inch deep. Plant three seeds per hole (thin the weakest ones if mother nature doesn't already). Plant in wide rows to make room for the vine, fruit, trellis, easy harvesting and airflow.

Growth Rate: Ranges greatly between variations, zucchini can be ready in a month or two, whereas some need all year to grow. The rule of thumb here is the larger the fruit, the longer it takes to grow, some needing four plus months.

Harvest: With most squash varieties you will be able to twist or cut the fruit off the vine. Since some varieties get so big with such a thick stem you might need help moving the fruit.

Yield: Zucchini plants might grow up to 50 fruits. Some squash and gourd varieties might do the same. You might choose to cut some fruit off bigger varieties of pumpkins and other show squash so that the plant can focus energy into a few fruits better.

Pros: Grows well. Large yield with often large fruit. Many very different varieties with many different uses. Satisfying to grow. Can be stored for a long time.

Cons: Takes up a lot of space, sometimes up to 25 feet of vine, plus fruit. Often a long growth period. Since the fruit is out so long it can be the target of many issues. Large fruit can't use trellis as efficiently without a base to grow on. Cross pollination with cucumbers and melons—even other squash—can turn your fruit into an unintended hybrid.

Companion Plants: ✓ Grows well by borrage, corn, peas, tomatoes and aromatic herbs. ✗ Avoid other other types of squash, cucumber, and melon. Also avoid beets, potatoes, cabbage family, broccoli, and onions.

Tips: You might use a tarp or garden canvas under the fruit to protect it from the ground. This won't be a perfect solution but will give it a better opportunity to grow as big as you want. You will absolutely need a trellis of some sort.

❂ Beans

Variations: When you think of growing beans in your garden, your first thought might be green beans, but snap peas, edamame, lima beans, and so on are all possible as well. Some beans have an edible pod like green beans, but some need to be cracked open so the peas can be removed and eaten. Bean pods are typically long and thin, but some can be much longer than others and range from green to yellow to red.

Growing Requirements

- Sun: Full sun, at least 8 hours
- Soil: Well drained soil, low fertility is fine
- Water: 2 inches a week, avoid getting plants wet

Sowing: Some bean plants might benefit from soaking the bean overnight. Plant the bean eye down. Bury the beans in 2 inches of soil. Plant in rows with access to a trellis. Make sure the rows are wide enough for you to fit through when harvesting.

Growth Rate: 1 ½ months.

Harvest: Pinch or cut the beans off the pole when they are the right size. A row of bean plants will put out multiple feedings of beans so harvest when there is a serving size and check daily for more. Make sure to bring a basket with you. For dried beans, some are left on the line to dry and picked then.

Yield: One plant equals about 30 beans.

Pros: Multiple feedings. Easy to grow. Large variety of beans. Possible multiple feedings per year. Adds nitrogen to the soil. Varieties like green beans can be eaten raw, cooked, or pickled.

Cons: Takes up a lot of space plus quick harvest leaves a lot of empty room if you are not going for a second harvest. Can be hard to organize and harvest.

Companion Plants: ✓ Grows well by squash, corn, cabbage family, cucumber, most root vegetables, anything that likes nitrogen, ✗ Avoid garlic, chives, onion, and leeks.

Tips: Prepare your trellis when planting. Beans get very spindly and need support. Unlike cucumber and squash that like to grow across the ground, beans love to have support.

BRANCHING/STALKS

✿ Celery

Variations: There are three variations of celery: celeriac, leafy, and pascal. Celeriac is more of a root vegetable growing like a turnip. Leafy celery is used as a herb for flavor. Pascal is the most popular and grown for the stalks. There are more sub variations of these three main types of celery.

Growing Requirements

- Sun: Full sun
- Soil: Rich, loose soil
- Water: Consistent moisture

Sowing: It's better to plant celery inside a few months before the last frost because of the long growth period. Plant up to ½ inch deep.

Growth Rate: Up to 4 ½ months with some quicker varieties.

Harvest: Cut off stocks when they are ready. Remove outer stocks, leave the inner stocks to keep growing. The very outer layer might need to be composted. Use clean sharp scissors.

Yield: One plant has about 10 stalks unless regular trimming.

Pros: High in nutrients. Dense plant. Can be preserved.

Cons: Celery is sensitive to the cold. Very long growth period. It needs a lot of nutrients.

Companion Plants: ✓ Grows well by beans, tomatoes, daisies, spinach, cosmos, onion, and cabbage family. ✗ Avoid corn and potatoes.

Tips: Prevent overcrowding when possible. Harvest before night's start to reach 50 °F.

✿ *Broccoli*

Variations: There are three main types of broccoli: purple cauliflower, calabrese, and sprouting. Purple cauliflower is the most popular with large floret heads and thick stems. Purple cauliflower comes in many colors. This is actually not the same as what we call cauliflower, which is part of a different family of plants. Sprouting broccoli has thinner stems but more heads. Calabrese is bluish with more branches.

Growing Requirements

- Sun: Full sun,
- Soil: Well-drained, very fertile
- Water: Likes the soil constantly moist

Sowing: Plant the seeds up to 1 inch deep but farther apart than most other plants, up to 1 foot. These plants can end up growing quite wide.

Growth Rate: 2 ½ to 3 ½ months.

Harvest: As the plant grows you will notice it starts to grow branches. Just before it flowers, take your scissors and cut off the branches that are ready.

Yield: One plant equals one head of broccoli.

Pros: High in nutrients. Freezes well. Hearty food. Might be able to fit a second harvest.

Cons: It can be really hard to time the harvest before your plant goes to flower at which point it is no longer desirable.

Companion Plants: ✓ Grows well by mint and dill, onions, sage, and rosemary. ✗ Avoid other squash, melon, and corn which all require a high dose of the same nutrients. Also avoid eggplant and potatoes.

Tips: Replenish soil after you grow broccoli because they can drain the soil for new years' plants.

✿ Tomatoes

Variations: Tomatoes might be the most popular food to find in a garden. That's partly because there are so many kinds of tomatoes from cherry tomatoes which are the size of a grape to beef steak which are up to 6 inches wide. They range in color as well from yellow, to classic red, to purple and pink. You can even get dwarf tomato plants if you are working with minimal space. There are a mindblowing 10,000 types of tomatoes.

Growing Requirements

- Sun: Full sun
- Soil: Well-drained, high nitrogen
- Water: Should be watered every day

Sowing: Most people do not plant tomatoes by seed, instead they buy tomato seedlings. Dig your hole an inch or so deeper than the root ball. This will provide the plant with a few more inches of support along the stem

Growth Rate: Depending on variety 2–3 ⅓ months.

Harvest: Twist the tomato off the plant, do not pull. You can do this when they are completely red, or even when they are still green. If they are just starting to blush it means they will not grow anymore, however waiting until they are red can improve their flavor. Green tomatoes can still turn red on the window sill, or be eaten as is. This can prevent an anticipated perfect tomato from being the target of nature's cruelty.

Yield: One can grow up to 300 cherry tomatoes to 30 large tomatoes.

Pros: Very versatile from soup, sauce, sliced, whole, on a sandwich to in your salad. Many different kinds. Very easy to grow. Fan favorite. Can be eaten before they are red.

Cons: Can be susceptible to disease including blight. Often too many tomatoes all at once. Attractive to pests. Not ideal for higher raised beds.

Companion Plants: ✓ Grows well by all herbs especially basil which improves flavor. Does well with squash and lettuce ✗ Avoid dill, potatoes, corn, fennel, and all cabbage family.

Tips: Plan your tomato support in advance. Tomatoes can get too big to get cages around, and then you will need another plan of action. Once they start producing fruit they get very top heavy. Once the fruit hits the ground they typically don't last very long. This support can also keep your tomatoes organized so you don't miss any and improves airflow.

✿ Hot Peppers/Bell Peppers

Variations: The pepper family is combined here because they grow the same, but the variation of peppers has its own cuisine niche. Hot pepper varieties are usually chosen for their level of hotness. Some of the most common are jalapeno, habanero, ghost, and cayenne. Sweet or bell peppers are fairly similar in taste with red being a little more sweet and green having a more distinct flavor.

Growing Requirements

- Sun: Full sun
- Soil: Well-drained, warm
- Water: Let dry slightly between waterings

Sowing: Like tomatoes, pepper plants are typically bought as seedlings and planted in the garden. Dig your hole an inch or so deeper than the root ball. This will provide the plant with a few more inches of support along the stem.

Growth Rate: 2–3 months.

Harvest: Twist or cut the pepper off the plant when it's ready. You can tell it's ready rather due to its length or its color.

Yield: One plant equals up to 10 for large bell peppers, and up to 50 for smaller sweet or hot peppers.

Pros: Intense flavor. Desirable texture. Colorful. High yield. Preserves well.

Cons: Takes up a lot of space. Not ideal for higher raised beds.

Companion Plants: ✓ Grows well by most herbs, eggplant, carrots, and squash ✗ Avoid all other members of the cabbage family

Tips: Some smaller plants might not need support or trellises, but the larger the fruit and taller the plant the more likely it is to become top heavy.

✿ Eggplant

Variations: There are 18 different types of eggplant. The globe eggplant is known as the classic eggplant which is long, smooth, and deep purple. The African eggplant is where the plant got its name since it looks like a normal egg growing out of a plant. The indian eggplant is short and red. There are cherry and pea varieties that are small and green like a grape. And other varieties that look more or less like the classic eggplant. The Globe eggplant is likely to be the variation that you will find in stores.

Growing Requirements

- Sun: Full sun, at least 6 hours
- Soil: Loose, well-drained, warm
- Water: 1 inch a week but may increase its need as the fruits get bigger

Sowing: Plant small seeds shallow, about ¼ of an inch deep. Plant at least 2–4 inches apart. Keep soil damp for the germination period.

Growth Rate: About 4 months.

Harvest: Once the eggplant is ready (based on variety), twist or cut them off the plant.

Yield: One plant equals up to six eggplants.

Pros: High in nutrients. Overall easy plant to grow. Large and interesting fruit.

Cons: Low yield, especially for long growth rate.

Companion Plants: ✓ Grows well by beans, peppers, leafy greens, and thyme ✗ Avoid fennel.

Tips: Use a trellis or some sort of support when the fruit gets big so the plant does not topple over from the weight.

✿ Asparagus

Variations: Up to 15 types of asparagus, the main ones are green, purple, white, and wild. Green is the most common and white is actually the same kind that is covered so it doesn't turn green. Purple is more tender. Wild asparagus is long and thin.

Growing Requirements

- Sun: Full sun, might tolerate partial shade, likes cool air
- Soil: Loose, well-drained, not acidic soil
- Water: Water deeply once a week

Sowing: Plant seeds shallow, about ¼ of an inch deep. Keep soil damp for the germination period. You can also transplant roots if you have some. They will grow for about two years, reach their peak at three and get smaller after that.

Growth Rate: Up to 10 inches a day

Harvest: Cut asparagus stocks at base of stock when they are about 10 inches long. Do not wait too long because they will keep growing into a herbaceous tree.

Yield: One plant equals one asparagus.

Pros: High in nutrients. Overall easy plant to grow. Kind of funny when it grows. Amazing growth rate.

Cons: Very small yield. Must be picked at the right time.

Companion Plants: ✓ Grows well by all herbs and can repel some tomato bugs. ✗ Avoid potatoes and garlic.

Tips: If you let asparagus grow to maturity one year without harvesting, the following year you will find more shoots growing in its place.

❀ Corn

Variations: There are six major types of corn however, most corn that is grown is actually used for livestock feed. Under these six major categories are thousands upon thousands of variations. The corn that most people have is sweet corn. Corn comes in many different colors and combinations of colors from blue to purple to red, orange, and so on. There are varieties that are grown specially for their jewel tones. The cob sizes also vary from 4 inches up to 12 inches.

Growing Requirements

- Sun: Full sun
- Soil: Well-drained, fertile

- Water: 1 inch a week, increases when it gets taller

Sowing: Plant the seeds 6 inches apart in rows that you can walk through. Plant at least four rows.

Growth Rate: About 4 months, sometimes on sunny days after a good rain you can hear the corn creak as it grows.

Harvest: Twist and pull the corn off the stalk when it's ready. Timing is important when picking corn. Pick when the husk is green but the silk (strings on the inside) are turning brown.

Yield: One plant equals one or two cobs.

Pros: Fun to grow. Can be a great companion plant for support. Home grown corn is the best tasting. Can be preserved in a pressure cooker, great filler.

Cons: Low yield, takes up a lot of space, can attract birds and other animals. Not ideal for higher raised beds.

Companion Plants: ✓ Grows well by beans, cucumbers, beets, most herbs, sunflowers, and amaranth ✗ Avoid other celery and tomatoes.

Tips: Prevent overcrowding when possible. It is encouraging to see lots of plants but long term can lose more by competition then by thinning.

FRUIT

When we think of most fruits, they grow in trees. This includes apples, peaches, bananas, nectarines, plums, pears, and so on. While this section is small, it lists four strong contenders you can grow in your garden. At the end of the plant definitions you will find a section on brambles which includes raspberries and blackberries and why they should not be grown in a raised bed. However, they are still a great addition to your garden somewhere else.

✿ *Strawberries*

Variations: There are over 600 types of strawberries. The wild strawberry is quite small compared to commercial strawberries. The June variety comes early and all at once. Day neutral variety produces over a longer period of time but less fruit. Varietes can affect color, size, sweetness, yield, bloom time, and period.

Growing Requirements

- Sun: Full sun
- Soil: Well-drained, highly fertile
- Water: High moisture when flower and fruiting, otherwise 1 inch per week

Sowing: Lightly spread the seeds over the ground and dust them with light soil and water deeply. Thin if needed.

Growth Rate: 1 to 1 ½ months.

Harvest: Pinch, twist, or cut berries off the plant when they look ready. Keep an eye out during their harvest period and harvest regularly because you don't want them to overripen.

Yield: One plant equals up to 20 strawberries if lucky.

Pros: Home grown strawberries are unanimously the best in flavor. Can be eaten fresh or in jams and other preserves. One of the few fruits not grown on fruit trees.

Cons: Very short season. Not a huge yield per plant.

Companion Plants: ✓ Grows well by flowers, beans, garlic, and leafy greens. ✗ Avoid all of the cabbage family, fennel, and turnips.

Tips: Plant flowers near strawberries that bloom at the same time to attract pollinators. Strawberries can be grown in pots too. Depending on variety you might need a trellis to add support.

✿ Blueberries

Variations: There are four main blueberry varieties, high and low bush, half high and rabbit eye. Highbush is the most popular because it is a reasonable height at a maximum 12 feet, and produces fruit fairly quickly. They are also desirable because they are the most resistant to bugs and disease which is even more important for a long term plant.

Growing Requirements

- Sun: Full sun but with shelter from elements
- Soil: Well-drained, acidic
- Water: Keep the ground wet

Sowing: Bushes can be planted in the spring or fall. More mature plants are ideal because they are stronger and more likely to produce higher yield of fruit. Plant these bushes away from each other to prevent competition.

Growth Rate: In their third year late spring to mid summer.

Harvest: Pluck berries off the bush when they are ready.

Yield: One established bush can have up to 450 berries, but often lower, especially for younger plants.

Pros: Produces every year. Yield increases every year. Can be made into jam and preserves.

Cons: Perennials and bushes are not the best addition to garden beds. Takes years before it is at its peak.

Companion Plants: ✓ Grows well by basil, borage, dill, and parsley ✗ Avoid plants that don't like acidic soil. Avoid plants that don't want blueberry bush shade or nutrient competition.

Tips: While the blueberry bush can survive in less than full sun, this will reduce the amount of fruit it produces.

✿ Melon

Variations: There are obvious variations of melon like watermelon, cantaloupe, and honey dew, but there are different kinds. If you are buying your seeds from a regular place however, these are the kinds you are most likely to find. You can also get mini versions of these plants which can be easier to grow. Each melon has its own look and taste. With most melons you can just take the seed from a fruit you ate and plant it.

Growing Requirements

- Sun: Full sun, at least 6 hours
- Soil: Loose, well-drained, fertile
- Water: High moisture, even more when fruits start appearing

Sowing: Plant seeds 4 inches apart and thin if necessary. Plant in rows so that you can access plants. Ideal to plant with trellis that can support and hold fruit. Plant about 1 inch deep.

Growth Rate: Up to 4 ½ months.

Harvest: Twist or cut fruit off the vine when it's ready. Ideal if the vine starts dying off to indicate peak harvest time.

Yield: One plant equals up to five melons on average. Cut away smaller ones to direct energy to the best if you think your plant is struggling.

Pros: Large, satisfying harvest. One of few fruits that are not grown from fruit trees.

Cons: Takes up a lot of space. Small yield. Cross pollination can ruin squash, cucumbers, and even other melons. Takes a long time to grow.

Companion Plants: ✓ Grows well by corn, pollinator flowers, and radishes. ✗ Avoid potatoes, other melon, squash, and cucumbers.

Tips: Like squash, if you can't get a supporting trellis, try adding a canvas or tarp under the fruit so that it is less susceptible to pests and diseases.

✿ Grapes

Variations: Over 10,000 types of grapes. They grow in woody vines and grow new leaves and fruit every year. Concord grapes are recommended for beginners. Grape varieties affect appearance, size, and flavor. Some grapes are grown for wine, but the grapes from your garden are most likely for eating so they should be a sweeter variety.

Growing Requirements

- Sun: Full sun
- Soil: Loose, well-drained, sandy, high potassium
- Water: Don't need a lot of water, rain should be enough unless there's a drought

Sowing: Plant a store bought seedling beside a fence or trellis. Ideal if your grapes are on the outside of your bed because of the amount of space. Adjust climbing direction to your liking as it grows. Prune when necessary.

Growth Rate: A three year old plant will start to produce grapes which will be ready in the late summer.

Harvest: When the grapes are ready, use a sharp pair of scissors to cut the cluster off the vine.

Yield: One plant equals about maximum 3,000 grapes or 40 grape clusters.

Pros: Low maintenance. High yield after maturity. Can be an attractive addition.

Cons: Takes up a lot of space. Takes a long time to mature. Not all grapes are edible. Can provide too much shade. Can creep and start killing other plants if not careful.

Companion Plants: ✓ Bean plants can help replenish soil. ✗ Avoid all leafy greens, in general avoid being too close to all vegetables.

Tips: If you use an arch for walking through for your treillis, the grapes can perfectly hang down towards you.

HERBS

Herbs are not usually eaten as a substantial part of a meal. They are used to add flavor to meals, or to be used as teas. Most of these herbs are also useful because they attract beneficial insects like ladybugs, parasitic wasps, and lace wigs and repel harmful bugs. Some people prefer to plant herbs in pots near a sitting area so they can enjoy the aromatic smells. Herbs are better picked earlier in the day to have the strongest scent.

✿ *Onion*

Variations: There are six main onion variations: red, yellow, green, white, leek, and shallot. A red onion is the strongest in flavor and has the largest bulb with a purple skin. A yellow onion tends to be the sweetest with a golden skin. A white onion is more mild but more crisp. A shallot is more mild and about ¼ the size of a red onion. A green onion is a small bulb with long shoots that are mild. A leek looks like a giant green onion and has a distinct leek flavor. They are used for different kinds of cooking.

Growing Requirements:

- Sun: Full sun, up to 13 hours
- Soil: Loose, well-drained, with organic material
- Water: 1 inch a week

Sowing: Plant onion bulbs in rows at least 2 inches a part. Plant the bulb with the roots down. Cover with 2 inches of soil.

Growth Rate: Up to six months.

Harvest: Pull out of the ground by the base of the stem. Move the first few layers of dirt off the top to check its the right size.

Yield: One plant equals one onion.

Pros: Used in most dishes to add flavor. Not very fussy. Stores well and can be pickled. Can act as a natural pesticide.

Cons: Hard to evaluate underground. Extremely long growth periods makes it inaccessible to grow in some places. Small yield.

Companion Plants: ✓ Grows well by beets, cabbage family, tomatoes, lettuce, and dill ✗ Avoid asparagus, sage, and peas.

Tips: Use a compassion plant even if you are not interested in harvesting onion to keep some pests away. Use the tops of onions for cooking as well.

✿ Garlic

Variations: There are 10 types of garlic which include: porcelain, rocambole, purple stripe, artichoke, silver skin, and creole. These are split into two categories: the hardneck and soft neck. Hardneck varieties are ideal for those with cooler winters and are claimed to have a stronger flavor. Softneck garlic is claimed to store longer and cook better. Despite the many kinds of garlic, the flavor is very similar in each case, so unless you have a favorite, pick the variety that you find the easiest to grow.

Growing Requirements

- Sun: Full sun
- Soil: Well drained, loose, and high fertility
- Water: 1 inch of water a week

Sowing: Plant a clove of your favorite garlic variety in the soil. If you are in growing zone 5 or less you can plant garlic in the fall around late October. Cover with a few inches of soil in rows.

Growth Rate: Usually nine months.

Harvest: Pull out of the ground by the base of the stem after the leaves start to turn yellow. Shake off any excess dirt. Use fresh or hang to dry so they store all winter in a cool dry place.

Yield: One plant equals one head of garlic.

Pros: Used in most dishes. Can grow enough to last a year. Stores well. Repels many pests.

Cons: Hard to evaluate underground. Very long growth period. Can be susceptible to diseases such as mold.

Companion Plants: ✓ Grows well by roses, cabbage family, tomatoes, lettuce, and potatoes ✗ Avoid peas and beans.

Tip: Can be used as bug repellent.

❀ Mint

Variations: There are over 600 varieties of mint. The most common varieties include peppermint which is used for teas and its scent, spearmint which is used as a flavoring additive to salads and desserts, chocolate mint which is used for drinks and desserts, mojito mint which is used for drinks, wild mint which is typically just used for herbal purposes.

Growing Requirements

- Sun: Full sun, might tolerate partial shade
- Soil: Loose, well-drained does not require high fertility
- Water: Likes average to slightly wet soil conditions

Sowing: Dig your hole an inch or so deeper than the root ball. This will provide the plant with a few more inches of support along the stem.

Growth Rate: 1–2 ½ months.

Harvest: Harvest regularly by trimming leaves and branches off mint. Pull out any mint spreading if you don't want it there. Cut off flowers to extend life.

Yield: One plant equals 10 branches with 20 leaves each approximately, but spreads like wildfire.

Pros: Grows really well, once you plant mint you will always have mint. Can be dried. Prevents bad bugs and attracts the good ones. Is used to help ease a upset stomach.

Cons: Mint grows like a weed and can spread across the whole garden, suffocating the other plants if you don't keep up with them.

Companion Plants: ✓ Grows well by almost everything in moderation and can add protection. ✗ Avoid parsley, and keep it from spreading too close to all plants.

Tips: Keep a note of the mint you plant. Since it is basically permanently in your garden, if you want to use it in the future it helps to know what kind of mint it is since different varieties have different purposes.

❁ Basil

Variations: Basil has a lot of variations and each variation can drastically affect the taste of the herb. There is a classic sweet basil, but also holy basil, red leaf basil, lemon basil, thai basil, and so on. If you are unsure which one you like, take a leaf from the store and smell and taste it. Licorice basil, for example, tastes more like fennel than the classic basil which would be a disappointment if you want basil.

Growing Requirements

- Sun: Full sun 6–8 hours
- Soil: Rich, organic, well drained
- Water: Deep watering once a week

Sowing: Basil is typically grown from store-bought seedlings and not a seed. Dig your hole an inch or so deeper than the root ball. This will provide the plant with a few more inches of support along the stem. Prune back enough so the plant does not get too long and lanky.

Growth Rate: About one month.

Harvest: As soon as the plant is established enough you can start cutting pieces off, but make sure you don't use too much and stunt the plant.

Yield: One plant has about 10–30 branches with about 10 leaves each.

Pros: Amazing flavor and repels a lot of harmful bugs.

Cons: Can be difficult to grow because it is fussy with too much and too little water. Must be deadheaded for flowers often, otherwise it will go to seed and die which can be a daily chore.

Companion Plants: ✓ Plant near tomatoes, asparagus, root vegetables, and peppers. Can help repel some pests ✗ Fennel, sage, and thyme.

Tips: Basil can also be grown in pots.

✿ Thyme

Variations: There are over 300 types of thyme. Not all of these are used for culinary purposes, but for the sake of simplicity those are the ones we will be discussing. Some of the most common are: english, french, caraway, lemon, and so on. English thyme is also called common or garden thyme and has a sharp flavor and many health benefits. French thyme is better in warmer climates and more mild. Caraway thyme is used for flavoring beef. Lemon thyme has a light taste and is used for poultry seasoning.

Growing Requirements

- Sun: Full sun and loves heat
- Soil: Loose, well-drained, with organic matter
- Water: Does not need much water, up to two weeks between watering

Sowing: Thyme is typically grown from store-bought seedlings and not a seed. Dig your hole an inch or so deeper than the root ball. This will provide the plant with a few more inches of support along the stem. Prune back enough so the plant does not get too long and lanky.

Growth Rate: Slow from seed, but once established can spread 12 inches in a month.

Harvest: Use a pair of scissors and snip off a few stems of thyme at a time. Deadhead when needed so the plant does not go to seed.

Yield: One plant equals up to a 12 by 12 inch plant with thin stems and small leaves.

Pros: Great flavor. Diverse varieties. Compact plant. Repels harmful bugs.

Cons: Avoid trying to grow from seed because it takes a long time and has an even lower success rate.

Companion Plants: ✓ Grows well by almost all plants and can enhance the flavor of the cabbage family. ✗ Avoid other herbs tend to like more water so they don't work best near each other.

Tips: Thyme typically crowd by creeping across the ground, so make sure it has enough space to expand.

❀ Rosemary

Variations: There are two main groups of rosemary. The first type grows as a small shrub and the other grows more like thyme by creeping across the ground. All varieties are edible, but some varieties are picked for more aromatic characteristics, yield, color, and so on, however the difference is not hugely impactful on the common gardener.

Growing Requirements

- Sun: Full sun, 6-8 hours
- Soil: Loose, well-drained
- Water: Deeply once a week in summer and every two weeks in the off seasons

Sowing: Rosemary is typically grown from store-bought seedlings and not a seed. Dig your hole an inch or so deeper than the root ball. This will provide the plant with a few more inches of support along the stem.

Prune back enough so the plant does not get too long and lanky.

Growth Rate: 3 ½ months if harvesting the whole plant.

Harvest: Trim off new growth whenever it's needed.

Yield: One plant equals up to 12 by 12 inch plant of dense needles.

Pros: Can be used for flavor. Easy to grow. Can be grown in a pot, even indoors. Has health benefits.

Cons: Weak against mold.

Companion Plants: ✓ Grows well by almost all plants especially the cabbage family, carrots, and beans ✗ Avoid mint plants including catnip

Tips: Trim your rosemary to encourage growth, but don't over prune or the plant might not recover.

✿ Dill

Variations: Dill is the seed produced from the plant, and the leaves from the plant are called dill weed. There are a few kinds of dill, however the range is smaller than many of the other plants. Bouquet is the most popular kind of dill plant and it is used in cooking for its aromatic quality. The other varieties range in size of plant and leaf.

Growing Requirements

- Sun: Full sun, at least 6 hours
- Soil: Loose, well-drained, acidic, organic matter
- Water: Keep the soil moderately moist

Sowing: Dill is typically grown from a store bought seedlings and not a seed. Dig your hole an inch or so deeper than the root ball. This will provide the plant with a few more inches of support along the stem. Prune back enough so the plant does not get too long and lanky.

Growth Rate: Three months.

Harvest: Trim off new growth whenever it's needed. Cut back the flower to prevent it going to seed if you want to get dill weed longer.

Yield: One plant equals a thin stem with small feathery branches and a few flower heads.

Pros: Great flavor. Overall easy plant to grow. Used in pickling. Attracts beneficial bugs.

Cons: Small yield. Lots of work to keep it from going to seed.

Companion Plants: ✓ Grows well by the cabbage family, corn, cucumbers, leafy greens, and nightshades. ✗ Avoid carrot and tomatoes.

Tips: Dill can get very tall and lanky so be careful when watering it so it does not snap or bend.

✿ Fennel

Variations: The entire plant of fennel is edible and it has a few main variations. Common fennel is both herb and vegetable. Sweet fennel is used exclusively as an herb. Bulb fennel is a vegetable. It is technically part of the carrot family.

Growing Requirements

- Sun: Full sun
- Soil: Loose, well-drained, with organic matter
- Water: About 1 inch a week

Sowing: Plant seeds shallow, about ½ of an inch deep. One seed per hole for newer seeds, double up if they are older. Plant at least 2–4 inches apart. Keep soil damp for the germination period.

Growth Rate: It will grow 2 feet the first year and 6 feet the next.

Harvest: Trim the greens off of the plant when needed for the herb. Pull out of the ground by the base of the stem when it looks the right size after brushing the top layer of dirt off the top.

Yield: One plant equals one bulb.

Pros: High in nutrients. Overall easy plant to grow. Saturated in flavor.

Cons: Hard to evaluate underground. Can be sensitive to improper conditions, especially soil. Can be targeted by carrot weevils and carrot rust fly as well as other common pests.

Companion Plants: ✓ Can have a negative effect on plants around them. Good for beneficial insects however.✗ Avoid eggplant, carrots, and most other plants.

Tips: You can plant fennel in your yard, even if you are not planting it in your garden with the rest of your plants.

✿ Parsley

Variations: There are four main types of parsley. Flat leaf parsley is used for its flavor. Curly leaf parsley is used the most often and is used for garnishes. Japanese parsley is eaten like celery. Humbergroot parsley is used for aesthetic purposes.

Growing Requirements

- Sun: Full sun, for 6 to 8 hours
- Soil: Loose, well-drained, rich
- Water: High moisture, keep moist

Sowing: Plant seeds shallow, about ¼ of an inch deep. One seed per hole for newer seeds, double up if they are older. Plant at least 2-4 inches apart. Keep soil damp for the germination period.

Growth Rate: Three months.

Harvest: Trim off new growth whenever it's needed.

Yield: One plant equals one head of parsley.

Pros: High in nutrients. Overall easy plant to grow. Attracts beneficial bugs.

Cons: Can be fussy with sun and water. Takes a little longer to grow then other herbs. Not necessarily hugely impactful.

Companion Plants: ✓ Grows well by most plants including carrots, onion, and tomatoes. ✗ Avoid mint.

❁ Oregano

Variations: Over 40 oregano variations, however they all have a similar flavor.

Growing Requirements

- Sun: Full sun means more flavor
- Soil: Loose, well-drained, sandy, organic matter
- Water: 1 inch a week, tolerant of drought.

Sowing: Plant seeds shallow, about ¼ of an inch deep or if grown from store-bought seedlings and not a seed. Dig your hole an inch or so deeper than the root ball. Plant at least 2–4 inches apart. Keep soil damp for the germination period.

Growth Rate: It takes 1 1/2 months.

Harvest: With scissors trim off the leaves as you need them. Prune when it starts to get overgrown.

Yield: One plant equals about two small stems of oregano.

Pros: High in nutrients. Overall easy plant to grow. Strong flavor. Small. Detracts harmful bugs.

Cons: Can be fussy with having enough sun.

Companion Plants: ✓ Grows well by cabbage family, dill, and asparagus. ✗ Avoid mint

FLOWERS

This section covers flowers to grow in your raised garden. These flowers are selected because they are edible, good companion plants for taste, pest repellent, and so on. All of these plants are edible which can give some relief when it comes to children, or even contamination.

✿ Pansies

Variations: There are over 500 kinds of pansies. The colors of pansies are endless with every color and color combination imaginable. Some of the pansies are grown to have longer stems to be more desirable in hanging baskets and urns. The clear pansy are solid colors. Usually their name is reference in which color and pattern they will grow into.

Growing Requirements

- Sun: Full sun or partial shade. Can be sensitive to harsh afternoon sun
- Soil: Loose, well-drained, fertile
- Water: Up to two times a day, especially if in full sun

Sowing: Plant seeds shallow, about ¼ of an inch deep. One seed per hole for newer seeds, double up if they are older. Plant at least 2–4 inches apart. Keep soil damp for the germination period. Plant in rows if you are planting many. Since they are low to the ground, they give them enough space to have airflow between plants.

Growth Rate: 1–2 months.

Harvest: Trim off the flower heads whenever you want to use them.

Yield: One plant equals up to 10 blooms over a period of time.

Pros: Edible flower. Overall easy plant to grow. Beautiful addition to the garden. Many colors. Attracts pollinators. Early bloomer. Doesn't take too much space.

Cons: Edible but not filling. Can not be cooked. Can attract slugs. Short harvest period.

Companion Plants: ✓ Grows well by almost leafy greens. Might do okay with squash if it doesn't swallow the plant completely. ✗ Avoid plants that will keep in too much moisture so it does not attract pests.

Tips: Deadhead flowers when they are dying off to encourage new flowers to grow.

✿ Nasturtium

Variations: All nasturtium varieties are edible. The plant usually flowers a yellow, red, and orange color palette with an array of patterns. However, white and peach varieties also occur. Some varieties will determine whether the plant prefers to climb or creep. If you have a preference, make sure to choose a variety that does the one you want. Some varieties can vary the shape of the flower, size of the flower and the plant, and so on.

Growing Requirements

- Sun: Full sun, might tolerate partial shade, but prefers up to eight hours of sun
- Soil: Loose, well-drained, prefers unfertile soil
- Water: Water when soil starts to dry

Sowing: File a thin layer of seed off one side to aid in germination. Plant about ¼ of an inch deep. Plant at least 2–4 inches apart. Keep soil damp for the germination period. Plan for large growth.

Growth Rate: 1–2 ½ months, flowers can be picked whenever blooming. Don't over harvest and kill the plant.

Harvest: Using a sharp and clean pair of scissors, cut off the desirable flowers and leaves.

Yield: One plant equals about 50 blooms and leaves if it is healthy.

Pros: Edible flowers and edible leaves that have a strong peppery flavor. Overall easy plant to grow. Beautiful bursts of color in the garden. Interesting round and large foliage. Deters harmful bugs. Pollinator.

Cons: Can take up a lot of room. Overpowering flavor might not be something that can be used very often. Not good for pets.

Companion Plants: ✓ Grows well by a family of cabbage, melons, and cucumbers. ✗ Can choke other plants so make sure to give them their room.

Tips: Nasturtium can be a ground crawler or be pulled up by a trellis. A trellis might make it more accessible to enjoy the flowers that can hide underneath its foliage.

✿ Sunflowers

Variations: All sunflowers have edible sunflower seeds. There is some debate on whether the petals are edible or not, but most say that they can be thrown in a salad. Most people prefer to grow large 'giant' or 'titan' variations because it is easier to get the seeds, and the seeds are larger. However sunflowers are a huge family and they range in all sorts of sizes. They can be grown also for ornamental value and range typically from yellow to orange, red, and purple.

Growing Requirements

- Sun: Full sun, at least six hours
- Soil: Loose, well-drained, very fertile with organic matter
- Water: 1 inch a week at least, more on hot days, check for wilting

Sowing: Plant seeds inch or two deep. One seed per hole for newer seeds, double up if they are older. Plant at least 2–4 inches apart. Keep soil damp for the germination period. You want it deep enough that it provides support.

Growth Rate: Giant sunflowers can grow 12 feet in 3 months, however smaller flowers grow about the same rate.

Harvest: Cut the flower off the stem when it starts to die. Remove the top later from the center, and underneath you will find the seeds densely packed. Put a basket under the flower as you pry the seeds out.

Yield: One plant equals 1–3 cups of seeds.

Pros: Overall easy plant to grow. Very beautiful. Many varieties to choose from.

Cons: Some plants can be very large and snap in half from the weight. Takes up alot of room for small yield. Not all varieties produce seeds.

Companion Plants: ✓ Grows well by corn, squash, and does well with most insert plant. ✗ Avoid mint and potatoes.

Tips: When growing large sunflowers they might need a support system. Sunflowers that produce seeds are very attractive; they can attract birds, rodents, and more so it can help to have a protection plan.

❀ Lavender

Variations: There are typically three types of lavender that you see, English, French and Spanish. There are more variations than this, and also variations of each of the common ones. Lavender can range from dark to light purple and even pink. English lavender is compared more to rosemary. French is compared more to pine. Spanish lavender is more about showing off its flowers. Since this is a perennial, some variations are more hardy in the snow.

Growing Requirements

- Sun: Full sun, prefers eight hours
- Soil: Lose, well-drained, does not require fertile soil
- Water: 1 inch a week, more on droughts

Sowing: Lavender is typically grown from a store bought seedlings and not a seed. Dig your hole an inch or so deeper than the root ball. This will provide the plant with a few more inches of support along the stem. Prune back enough so the plant does not get too woody.

Growth Rate: Six months.

Harvest: Gather the bushel of lavender with a string and use sharp scissors to cut across the bottom.

Yield: One plant equals one bouquet.

Pros: Very nice scent. Edible. Perennial. Can repel harmful bugs. Helps aid in falling asleep. Used in desserts to add floral taste.

Cons: Can become woody. Can grow very slowly. Edible but not filling. Small yield. Might not be hearty enough to survive harsh winters.

Companion Plants: ✓ Grows well by most plants especially basil. Can help out the cabbage family as well. Might add some shade to plants behind it. ✗ Avoid trees that provide shade.

Tips: Lavender grows best in the heat and full sun so don't be shy when planting. Can be dried and used for its scent.

❀ Roses

Variations: Roses come in all shapes and sizes. Which variation you want depends on why you are looking to plant your roses. If you are looking for the best edible roses, dog rose, a type of wild rose is often called the best. If you are looking for ornamental roses, you can get big beautiful roses bushes or tiny dwarf bushes that fit in your raised bed. Roses come in many different colors, prominently pink and red, but also white and yellow. Your rose bush variation can affect the shape the bush takes on too. Wild roses tend to have less appealing bushes and become lanky. Ornamental trees are more dense with a deeper green.

Growing Requirements

- Sun: Full sun, minimum four hours.
- Soil: Loose, well-drained, adaptable
- Water: 2 inch a week

Sowing: Roses can be grown from seed but is typically grown from store-bought seedlings. Dig your hole an inch or so deeper than the root ball. This will provide the plant with a few more inches of support along the stem. Water deeply. Plant with other rose bushes to create a denser bush.

Growth Rate: It can take years for roses to reach their maximum height, but after about two or three years they will start blooming.

Harvest: With scissors and being careful with the thorns, clip the head of the rose off. If you just want the petals, gently pull off the petals and leave the center so a rosehip can be used later. Wait until the rosehip has had a light frost to sweeten them. They should still be firm.

Yield: One plant equals up to 1–500 blooms depending on the variation. Rose hips grow wherever flowers bloom.

Pros: Overall easy plant to grow. In your raised bed a rose bush can attract pollinators and other beneficial bugs. Roses are used in tea, desserts, and beauty. Absolutely stunning flowers and scent. Rosehips can be used too.

Cons: Very short bloom time. Takes up a lot of space unless pruned or dwarfed. Not a filling harvest.

Companion Plants: ✓ Grows well by beets, the cabbage family, leafy greens, as well as radishes. ✗ Avoid plants with opposing requirements, fuchsias, and other bushes.

Tips: Use a thick pair of rubber gloves when working with a rose bush to prevent being struck by the thorns.

✿ Daisies

Variations: Daisies is a big family of flowers, most of which look fairly similar to each other. The most common daisy in the garden is the chamomile flower. The chamomile flower can be used as an herb or for making teas. Many other variations of daisies are edible, but some more so than others. Chamomile has a different foliage then the classic sasha or oxeye daisies which are technically edible, but not exactly tasty. Chamomile has a feathery dill-like foliage instead.

Growing Requirements

- Sun: Full sun, eight plus hours if possible
- Soil: Loose, well-drained, sandy, but rich
- Water: 1 inch a week, 2 inches if it's hot

Sowing: Daisies are perennials, so regardless if they are planted by seed or seedling they come back every year. Chamomile might have difficulty if the garden is being turned over every year however.

Growth Rate: Some are biennials that will bloom the second year unless planted as a seedling.

Harvest: Cut of blooms as they come. Oxyeye varieties have one bloom per stem but chamomile has many small blooms over a period of time. Dry them if you want.

Yield: One plant equals 1–25 blooms.

Pros: Overall easy plant to grow. Beautiful addition to the garden and food. Comes back every year.

Cons: Hard to rely on. Small yield. Not a lot of common uses unless you drink a lot of tea.

Companion Plants: ✓ Grows well by onions and attracts beneficial bugs ✗ Avoid plants with opposing requirements.

Tips: Plant new daisy seeds once every few years to top up dwindling populations.

✿ Daylilies

Variations: Despite the name, the daylily is not actually a lily. It might also be called the tiger lily, although this is generally incorrect and shares a name with an actual lily. You can tell it is not an actual lily from its foliage. The leaves on a daylily all start at the base of the stem and point up into a V shape. The lily family has leaves that grow straight out all the way up the stem with shorter leaves. Daylilies can vary in color, from yellow to red but are typically orange. They grow from a bulb underground. Unless you are absolutely confident in your identification do not eat, because all lilies are poisonous.

Growing Requirements

- Sun: Full sun, at least six hours a day
- Soil: Loose, well-drained, rich soil
- Water: 1 inch a week, rain should be enough

Sowing: Bury the bulb 2–3 inches in the ground, in a placement that you desire. Give the bulbs enough space to grow over the years.

Growth Rate: Three to four years.

Harvest: The flowers are edible, and can be cut off when they are blooming. The root is also edible and can be dug up once the season is over if you want. The root must be peeled and can be cooked the same as a potato.

Yield: One plant equals 1–4 blooms.

Pros: Comes back every year. Is a beautiful addition to the garden. Is edible. Attracts pollinators.

Cons: Takes up a lot of space. Not a filling harvest.

Companion Plants: ✓ Grows well by most plants, specifically flowering plants.✗ Avoid plants with opposing requirements.

Tips: Harvest the blooms as you see them because they close at night. Plant strategically because these plants will come back over again.

✿ Yarrow

Variations: Over 50,000 yarrow variations. Yarrow is also known as alyssum. It looks similar to a wild carrot with a much denser floret. The little flowers that make up the floret come in white, peach, yellow, pink, and beige. The plant itself varies very little with dark green feathery foliage.

Growing Requirements

- Sun: Full sun, might tolerate partial shade
- Soil: Loose, well-drained, sandy or loamy
- Water: Drought tolerant once it's mature. Rain is likely enough, supplement if needed

Sowing: Plant seeds shallow, about ½ of an inch deep. One seed per hole for newer seeds, double up if they are older. Plant at least 2 inches apart. Keep soil damp for the germination period. They are perennials and come back every year.

Growth Rate: Three to four months.

Harvest: Unless you are using the yarrow for decoration or herbal use you probably won't be harvesting it. If you simply cut it, use clean, sharp scissors.

Yield: One plant equals about 10–20 flower stalks.

Pros: Yarrow is not used for eating, although it is technically edible. It is however used in a lot of herbal medicine. It is a beautiful addition to the garden.

Cons: In large amounts it can be poisonous.

Companion Plants: ✓ Grows well as a pollinator and repels some pests. Can help tomatoes, the cabbage family, spinach, all herbs, and beans. ✗ Avoid planting too much because it can be poisonous in large amounts.

Tips: As a medium size plant it fills a space pretty well. It may not be the first pick for a raised bed, but it is an easy to care for plant that gives a few benefits. It is safe to have near food and kids.

❀ *Borage*

Variations: There are four types of borage. The most popular is common borage. It grows about 3 feet tall and has many small blue flowers. The next kind is a variegated version of the previous plant, so the leaves are just white. Alba is a version with white blooms and later bloom time. Creeping borage crawls across the ground instead of growing tall.

Growing Requirements

- Sun: Full sun, might tolerate partial shade
- Soil: Loose, well-drained, sandy, low nutrients
- Water: High moisture, likes to be constantly wet

Sowing: Plant shallow, about ¼ of an inch deep. You might be able to just sprinkle the leaves on top. One seed per hole for newer seeds, double up if they are older. Plant at least 2–4 inches apart. Keep soil damp for the germination period.

Growth Rate: 1 ½ months.

Harvest: You can harvest the flowers as they come, and clip off leaves if you want to eat them.

Yield: One plant equals 100 small flowers and a bushel of leaves.

Pros: Is good for the soil. Overall easy plant to grow. Has pretty flowers and is edible.

Cons: Not the most desirable foliage since it is spiky, and not the most attractive flower.

Companion Plants: ✓ Grows well with most plants and repels harmful bugs. Plant with tomatoes, the cabbage family, and strawberries. Attracts pollinators. ✗ Avoid very contrasting plant requirements.

Tips: Borage can get long and start to drag on the ground. If you add minor support like stakes you can keep the plants off the ground and keep the leaves and flowers fresh for harvest.

❀ Marigolds

Variations: There are about 60 variations of marigolds. The variation in plants can drastically change the flower you will get. African marigolds, for example, are very short and dense flowers. They are only about 6 inches off the ground, with thick stems and 5 inch wide blooms that are dense with blooms similar to a peony. The french marigold on the other hand looks more like a large buttercup with a long dainty stem. They are typically orange, rusty red or yellow. Calendula is often referred to as the pot marigold.

Growing Requirements

- Sun: Full sun, might tolerate partial shade
- Soil: Loose, well-drained, highly fertile

- Water: Deeply once a week, more during the heat

Sowing: Plant seeds shallow, about ¼ of an inch deep. Keep soil damp for the germination period. Also you might buy marigolds as seedlings from the store. Dig your hole an inch or so deeper than the root ball. This will provide the plant with a few more inches of support along the stem. Water deeply. Plant with other rose bushes to create a denser bush.

Growth Rate: 1 ½ months.

Harvest: Marigolds are often planted for their beneficial nature in the garden, but if you want to eat them, clip them when the blooms are ready. Only some varieties are edible.

Yield: One plant equals 1–5 blooms.

Pros: Overall easy plant to grow. Their colors are eye-catching in the garden. They attract good bugs and deter bad ones. Often planted to repel mosquitoes.

Cons: Not the most edible, and should only be eaten in moderation.

Companion Plants: ✓ Grows well by almost every plant and is beneficial to them. ✗ Avoid planting near beans.

Tips: Prevent overcrowding when possible. It is encouraging to see lots of plants but long term can lose more by competition then by thinning.

WHAT (MAYBE) NOT TO GROW

The following section is not a definitive list of plants not to grow in a raised bed. If you have your heart set on any of these options then follow your heart. However, these are plants or plant types that I would not recommend for the following reasons.

Trees: Trees are a great resource in your backyard from pines that provide shade to fruit trees. They are better in the ground than a raised garden bed. They take up too much space and they will become too big and heavy for the bed which can make them unstable and eventually become a safety hazard.

Brambles: Brambles include plants like raspberry and blackberry bushes. They are usually like a long unruly vine that also often has thorns. This might be a great addition to the outside of your fence, but in a raised garden it takes up too much space.

Invasive: This might sound like an obvious statement not to plant invasive plants but plants like mint can take over very quickly. You may also not realize how invasive a plant really is. If you like a lot of mint then this might be ideal for you, but before you plant something make sure that it is not going to be detrimental to your soil or even spread to your local environment and take over.

Plants not right for your garden: There are plants in this chapter that are listed that are great garden plants but are not going to be right for your garden. If you are working with a small space then growing a squash vine is probably not going to work. If the squash doesn't take over completely, overcrowding might cause water to linger longer and cause mold or attract pests like snails. You should take your specific circumstances into consideration before planting things.

Plants not right for your area: Some plants that are not native to an area can still grow as long as it is planted at a time where there is no danger or frost. If you are planting make sure that you know your zone and the ideal zone for the plants. Even if a plant excels for a few summer months it might not be compatible with the length of the season and might die before it gets to fully produce.

Space and Numbers: You might pick some plants off this chapter for your garden but some plants need to be planted in higher numbers to get a worthwhile yield. The opposite might happen and planting too many gives you an unnecessary surplus of harvest. When planting you should be considering if you plan to preserve and how much you will need for a recipe or for your ideal stockpile.

PLANNING TO PLANT

It can be helpful to make a list of the plants you intend to grow and make a note of their necessary minimum temperature and when that will approximately be in your area, how long it takes to fruit and when that will be (this will differ if you are seeding indoors/ buying plants or sowing straight into the ground). This will help you determine whether your plant plan is going to be successful. It can also help you stagger harvests or for fast growing plants like lettuce plan for two harvest times.

5

PLANTING AND MAINTAINING

Once your garden plans are confirmed and the beds are set, it's time to start planting. When you are planting remember to plant or sow at a distance that is going to be optimal for the full sized plants to spread out. If you are sowing seeds straight in the ground you might want to go back later and remove the less successful seedings. This way you make sure the successful plants don't have competition because all of the seeds may not germinate.

If you are sowing seeds, check the package or look up the depth the seeds require. Some seeds need to be planted deeper to give it more support. For other plants they might require only a sprinkling because they are not strong enough to push through heavy dirt.

For seedlings and more established plants it is a good idea to dig the hole and water the hole before setting the root ball in. Most people are planting during the day in the bright sun and this will allow for deep watering without getting the rest of the plant wet. Seedlings should also be deeply watered to start germination as well. Some seeds might even benefit from being soaked in a glass of water beforehand. The seeds that are floating in the morning are likely to be dead.

When planting seedlings, dig the hole a few inches deeper than the rot ball. Unlike planting straight in the ground where the gardener might need to make room to add good dirt, a raised bed is already filled with good dirt. The reason to dig a little bit more room for the seedlings is so to add a few more inches of support to the stem. This is especially necessary with plants like tomatoes that can end up a bit lanky.

WATER

Watering the garden is not the same as watering indoor plants. There is a lot of emphasis for indoor plants not to overwater. Raised garden beds have much more dirt and are outside in the sun so there is less of a worry about overwatering. If the raised bed is lined with plastic it means that the water is going to be held there until it evaporates or the plants use it. The water sitting on top of the lining will change your watering routines. Using a hose uses much more water then other watering methods and can flood the bed. Watering isn't just about following a schedule, you have to use some intuition to see what the plants need. If it has been raining a lot you probably can pass watering for a while. If your plants are wilting and it isn't because of too much water, then water. If you stick your finger in the soil and the first few inches are dry that's a good indication that it times to water.

If you have a water softener it can have a negative effect on plants by depositing salt. If possible you can hook up your hose connection to the water system before it reaches the softener.

You should also water your plants in the evening. This prevents the sun from creating burns from the water drops. On days where you predict a heat wave you might choose to water early in the morning so that the plants that don't excel in the heat don't wilt past the point of no return during the day.

Soaker hoses often get clogged, crack, and don't always water evenly. The benefit is that they are convenient. With the proper head for your hose you are able to have more control about where the water goes and how much.

Watering cans can be inconvenient because of their small size. It can mean lugging aheavy watering can around which might not be accessible to everyone. However, they are a good option because you can fill them up to let the water sit and burn off anything that might be in the water and adjust to a warmer temperature. They are also a great option for a more controlled/accurate fertilization. However, depending on the space you have to water you might need multiple watering cans.

Sprinklers in the garden can encourage and spread disease by getting the leaves wet. Like a hose spraying water results in excess evaporation and doesn't always reach the soil and evenly moisten the root zone. On the other hand, sprinklers are a good option for convenience. Watering your plants can take up a lot of time every day and a sprinkler can work on those days where you just don't have the time.

Drip lines water the soil, not the plant. Drip lines also provide water at an even rate, allowing the soil to absorb the moisture with minimal waste or evaporation. The negative side is that it is hard to tell if they are working or broken. If you have plants that don't like constant water it is not the optimal option.

How Often Should You Water a Raised Bed Garden?

Watering frequency is an important factor when maintaining a raised bed garden. When choosing how often to water your plants, consider these factors:

Region: If you live in a dry region, you will need to water your raised bed as often as possible to keep the soil moist. If you live in a rainy region, you will have to water your raised bed less often.

Season: In dry seasons like summer, you should water your raised beds regularly. In the fall, you should consider the rain while watering your raised bed to avoid overwatering.

Plants: The plants in your raised bed determine how often you should water them. Plants such as tomatoes and cucumbers require more water than root vegetables such as potatoes and radishes.

Water Drainage Quality: If your raised bed drains water easily, you will need to water it more often. Never allow the soil to become fully dry.

FERTILIZER

Fertilizer is a compound added to your soil to add nutrients; as the name implies it is intended to make your garden more fertile. Just like soil, fertilizers are not all the same. Fertilizer comes in many forms, from a liquid concentrate, to salt-like rocks, to a solid bar. You should pick your fertilizer based on the plants you grow and where you live. With a raised bed you will have to worry about balancing out your local soil less, but it will still have an effect on your garden. If you are planting in the ground, it is even more important to use a fertilizer to balance your soil. One way to know what your soil needs is by buying a test kit. This will give you accurate results.

As we started in Chapter 3 on the composition of soil, the substances that soil needs are nitrogen, oxygen, carbon, phosphorus, and potassium. The minerals that they need which are secondary are calcium, sulfur, and magnesium. When we think about fertilizer, we want to replace any of the nutrients that are low. Nutrients might be low simply over time, or you might have a plant that requires more or less of some substances.

In addition to using fertilizer, you might also consider the pH of your soil. If your soil is acidic, meaning a lower pH, you can add lime which is very basic. If your soil is basic you can add coffee ground or pine needles which are very high in acidity. If you have sandy soil it is likely acidic, and clay soil leans more towards alkaline. Just like with their nutrients, different plants prefer different pH levels. If you can, you might plant plants with like needs near each other. So, mulch will add in organic components that hold water, and nutrients better, the pH is balanced by adding an acid or a base, and fertilizer adds back in the nutrients. All of this combined creates a strong foundation for fantastic fruit and flowers.

How and When to Fertilize?

Figuring out when to fertilize can be tricky. The first thing to check is what each plant recommends. Some plants prefer less fertile soil and adding too much can actually burn their roots. One option is to buy a test kit. It is also a good idea to get familiar with the plants you have. Plants like tomatoes for example can suck the nitrogen out of the soil so it is likely that they will need a more nitrogen heavy fertilizer more often, whereas corn takes away a lot of potassium. This is often why farmers rotate crops, so not to have a single plant ruin the composition of the soil.

The benefit of using store-bought fertilizer is that it is labeled with its composition. This takes out a lot of the guesswork. When it comes to organic fertilizers it can be hard to truly measure what you are adding to the soil. However, when making your own compost, you are able to customize to your liking more. If you know you need more calcium, you can add eggshells, thus creating a composition specifically made for your garden's needs. More about compost and fertilizer in Chapter 3.

Store-bought fertilizer comes with instructions and dosage which is also quite useful. The three main forms that it comes in is as a liquid concentrate in a dropper bottle, a salt-like concentrate, and a solid slow release form. There are also different methods of applying the fertilizer. For a larger area there is a hose end option that disperses the fertilizer, although the accuracy is very low. It also gets a lot of fertilizer on the plants which can cause burning. Adding either concentrate into water and applying with a watering can is accurate and allows the nutrients to reach the roots almost instantly, but again make sure to not get any on the plant above ground. Slow release fertilizer can come in pellets or larger sticks. They can be useful in plants that like a lot of nutrients, but many plants don't want constant nutrients. They can also be unreliable because they can release too quickly or wash away. The benefit is it can reduce the amount of work for you which is almost always worth it.

Don't just fertilize because you think you should. Too much fertilizer is not good for the plants or the garden. Very fertile soil can attract pests, which will be discussed below.

TROUBLESHOOTING: PESTS, MOLD, AND DISEASE CONTROL

Pests are not something you can predict, but it is important to keep an eye out for these pests or add preventative measures so that they don't get worse. One of the problems with pests is that they might seem like not a big deal when you first notice them but over time they get worse and they damage the plants until the plants are dead.

✿ Aphids

Identify: They vary in color from green, orange, brown, and white. They are small, and without a cluster you might not notice them at all. If you notice the leaves of your plants are looking disformed or yellow, look under the leaves for them. There might be a sticky substance. Aphids like nasturtium and sunflowers though they aren't necessarily picky.

Treatment: You might start your treatment by spraying your plants down with a heavy stream of water. If you don't mind using a pesticide, use an insecticidal soap aimed for aphids. There are insecticidal soaps that do qualify under organic gardens. Always do a spray test on the plant before you spray anything on it, and leave it 24 hours to make sure that it won't kill the plant. Consider releasing ladybugs in your garden which is a beneficial bug that will eat the aphids. Planting onions, garlic, and smelling plants can also repel them. Always plan to spray in the evenings so there is no direct sun on the wet plant.

✿ *Whitefly*

Identify: Whiteflies are small soft-bodied white flies, which are about half the size of a black fly. They like the underside of new leaves. You might not notice them until you knock into the plant and they go flying. Leaves might turn yellow and dry. They like most vegetables such as tomatoes, potatoes, corn, and cabbage, but can infest anything.

Treatment: It can be hard to tame an infestation of whiteflies because they are fast fliers and can move from one plant to the next. It can be beneficial to simply remove the plant that is having the issue if it is localized enough. Bringing in predators like lacewings can help control the population. Putting shiny or reflective substances near the plants might repel them. If you turn to a pesticide, always do a spray test on the plant before you spray anything on it, and leave it 24 hours. Always plan to spray in the evenings so there is no direct sun on the wet plant.

❀ Mealybug

Identify: Mealybugs are small white beetle-like bugs. They have an almost fluffy appearance to them and leave a fuzzy white residue behind. A mealybug will leave a bright orange residue when squashed. They like to hide in the smallest seams of a plant. The plant might look disformed or yellow. They like lots of nitrogen in the soil and soft plants.

Treatment: Removing them by hand might work if the issue is small enough. They will be killed immediately with a q-tip and a solution of water and hydrogen peroxide. A common predator to mealybugs is the parasitic wasp as well as ladybugs and lacewings. Mealy bugs can be hard to control with insecticides, so try other methods first.

❀ Thrips

Identify: Thrips are very, very small. They have long, yellow, green and even brownish bodies. Because they are so small it can be very hard to notice them unless the infestation is severe. If you see that there is damage to your plant, try shaking a branch or leaf onto a white background to get a better look.

Treatment: A good place to start with treating thrips is by spraying the plant with a very strong stream of water. Yellow and blue colored sticky traps can be set. If you turn to a pesticide, always do a spray test on the plant before you spray anything on it, and leave it 24 hours. Always plan to spray in the evenings so there is no direct sun on the wet plant.

✿ Hornworm

Identify: The hornworm is a thick, bright green caterpillar. It can best be identified by its love of tomatoes. It will often be found near tomato plants. They are rather large and can be almost surprising because of how big they are, yet they blend into plants fairly well.

Treatment: You might start by picking the bugs off and squishing them. They are large enough you might be able to control them this way. If the problem escalates, a soap and water spray is the next step. Just like stronger insecticides, it is important to do a spray test on your plants even if a small amount of dish soap can kill them.

✿ Japanese Beetle

Identify: Japanese beetles are about the size of a wasp, with a bright green head and with a brown back. They can fly, and when a plant is disturbed you might notice them flying out of the plant. They can be spotted matting on the leaves of plants. The leaves might show signs of damage with holes or even turning brown and dying.

Treatment: One option for collecting the beetles is a bag that is connected to a hormone or scent that the Japanese beetles are attracted to. These bags are designed to let the beetles fall in but makes it hard for them to escape. If you can stomach it, you can also crush up the dead bugs and spray the perimeter of the garden which can deter them from coming back. Besides this a spray of soap and water, or pesticide will work. Always plan to spray in the evenings so there is no direct sun on the wet plant.

✿ Slugs

Identify: Slugs like damp places, so it is likely that if you have a lot of low lying plants that keep moisture in they are more likely to appear. Slugs are typically 1–3 inches long with fleshy bodies. A great indicator a slug has been around is if you notice their shiny slime trail around on leaves. They cause damage like holes in leaves, causing the leaf and plant to die.

Treatment: Removing any excess cover over the ground where the slugs can be hiding. Reducing the amount you are watering, at least until the problem dies down, can help. Crush any egg clusters you find.

Adding coffee grounds, copper wire, and other barriers can prevent your slugs from approaching your plants. Slugs are not fans of aromatic plants, so that can work as a preventative measure. Lots of homemade spray remedies work on slugs because their skin is thin, including vinegar or ammonia mixed with water. Do a spray test on your plants even if a small amount of dish soap can kill them.

✿ Cabbage Looper

Identify: As the name implies, the cabbage looper can be found on cabbage plants and other plants that are similar like broccoli, leafy greens, tomatoes, and the tops or root vegetables. The cabbage looper is a caterpillar, bright green, but thinner than the hornworm. Their damage on plants can be identified as holes in the leaves.

Treatment: Cabbage looper does not like thyme, but loves mustard. You can use thyme to repel, or mustard to distract. The Farmers Almanac also recommends covering the plant being targeted with rye or cornmeal, which will cause the insect to eat and then to swell and die. Lastly, you can always use a pesticide.

✿ Fire Ants

Identify: There are many kinds of ants and many of them are actually beneficial to your garden. Other types of ants like black ants are predators and can reduce the amount of unwanted bugs. If there are too many ants it can start to cause problems. Fire ants on the other hand are not great friends. For starters they get their name because their bite feels like a burn. They also can cause damage to your plants. They are smaller than typical black ants and a bright orange color. Even if they are not damaging your garden, their removal makes harvesting and care easier.

Treatment: Many aromatic herbs will repel fire ants as a preventative measure. If you can find the ant's hole, you can try flooding it, some people even recommend filling it with boiling water. Don't use this method too close to your garden because the hot water can harm the roots. They might be repelled from hot spice. For a homemade spray, you might try adding citrus essential oil to water and spraying it on the ants. Lastly, you can always use a pesticide.

✿ *Gophers, Moles, and Voles*

Identify: One of the reasons that farmers traditionally didn't like gophers and the like is because the holes in the field could cause a horse to break its leg, but they can be a nuisance in the home garden as well. You can identify if a mole/gopher/vole is your problem if you notice any raised piles of dirt in your yard or garden. Even if they are not eating your plants, they can be disrupting the plants and causing trauma to the roots.

Treatment: These animals might be in your garden because they have a surplus of food which includes a variety of bugs. If you are able to identify this source and remove it they might leave as well. Adding tastes that they don't like around like garlic or spice can deter them as well as marigolds. If the problem is really severe you might need to consider setting traps.

✿ Chipmunks, Mice, Rats, Birds, Deer, Rabbits and More

Identify: The reason all of these animals are clumped together is because while they are all very different animals, their damage and defense is fairly similar. All of these animals will be eating a larger amount of the plant. If you can identify which animal is causing the damage then you can more specifically create a defense.

Treatment: If you are dealing with damage from an animal at night, you can add a light around your garden to deter it. A motion detection light can even work better because it can spook the animal away. A fence around the garden can work to keep most of these animals out as long as they are tall enough, with small enough wire patterns, and a secure bottom seam to prevent burrowing under. For animals that can climb and fly this is not going to help much. If these animals are causing enough problems you might need to build the fence tall enough to comfortably stand under and add a wire roof as well. For smaller animals you might want to set traps or use a BB gun. There are products that use different scents to deter animals. Avoid leaving food out for animals like bird seeds or even keeping compost too close to the garden. Try adding tastes that they don't like around like garlic or hot spice.

✿ *White Mold/Powdery Mildew*

Identify: White mold is fairly common in gardens. It looks like small-medium size patches of white. You may not notice it at first but it spreads. The reason it is often called powdery mildew is because it does not necessarily resemble the classic fuzzy mold look. It looks more like someone sprinkled icing sugar on a leaf. Powdery mildew is a fungal infection, which is important to know when it comes to treatment.

Treatment: The cause of white mold is having very little air flow with high moisture content rather than water or humidity. If you are able to cut away from foliage without doing too much damage it can allow more air flow. A common treatment is 1 tbsp of baking soda to 1 gallon of water and spray it on your leaves in the evening after a patch test.

✿ *Black Spot*

Identify: Black spot is a fungus that starts off as small veiny patches on the leaves of your plant. The patches are dark in color but might appear more reddish. Often you will also see a rim of yellowing leaf around the patch of fungus. It is most common to see roses with black spots but any plant that is similarly herbaceous can be affected.

Treatment: The treatment for black spot can start with a home remedy like the one for white mold; 1 tbsp of baking soda to 1 gallon of water and spray it on your leaves. However, you might have to go for a stronger fungicide for this culprit.

✿ Blight

Identify: Blight is the symptom of rapid decay of tissue, but it can be caused by many diseases, fungi, or pests. Blight can unfortunately be easy to spot because of how rapidly it can spread through your plant. The leaves will start to turn yellow and the leaves and fruit will start to develop dry circular brown patches. Mildew and rust are included in types of blights. Some of the specific blights that gardeners worry about are different tomato blights that are all fungal and potato blight.

Treatment: Avoid any damage to your plants because blight enters through injuries. If you notice blight starting, remove the affected parts of the plant in hopes the rest of the plant and crop don't catch it. Don't water the plant from the top, the water droplets can spray spores around and spread the issue. Take any damaged part of the plant far away from your garden so that it can not spread.

✿ *Downy Mildew*

Identify: Downy mildew looks like yellow patches of dying leaf. These patches are small but can cluster. Downy mildew attacks from under the leaf and eventually kills it. It affects plants like sunflowers and pansies, but many more. It climbs up the plant from the soil.

Treatment: Similar to that of white mold, start by allowing more air flow. A common treatment is 1 tbsp of baking soda to 1 gallon of water and spray it on your leaves in the evening after a patch test.

✿ *Rust*

Identify: Rust is a type of fungal disease. The reason for its name is because the bright orange fungus looks almost identical to metal rust. The plant might start off with a few small dots of orange that will progress into a large patch surrounded by yellow dying foliage. It is common in many plants. Do not water the plants from the top, this encourages growth and spread.

Treatment: If you can remove the affected pieces from the plant, start there and make sure to dispose of it properly. If the problem is larger than a leaf or two you can try the spray used for powdery and downy mildew. You may also try neem oil which is an organic oil that has been proven to kill fungus. Sulfur can be used as a treatment or a commercial fungicide.

6

HARVEST YOUR GARDEN

Harvesting the garden is one of the most satisfying parts of gardening. Not every plant will be ready to harvest at the same time and the same way. When we think of 'harvest' time, images of autumn, baling wheat fields, Thanksgiving, and so on are common. Some plants are harvested in that image. They need all season to develop such a large vegetable.

For other plants they need to be harvested regularly throughout the season otherwise they will stop producing because they have finished their life cycle. Knowing the right time to harvest is essential. Without proper timing you might overzealously pick before its ready which might make it inedible or at the very least more bitter. Letting the fruit stay on the plant longer can improve the taste, but it does run the risk of over-ripening or being the target of pests.

WHEN IS IT TIME TO HARVEST YOUR VEGETABLES?

In Chapter 4 under each plant there is an approximate time for when they are ready for harvest. This is an estimate because under different climates and conditions plants will grow differently. Instead of giving an estimated date or month, it just gives a time frame after planting. This is because the planting date ranges for many depending on the last frost. Some plants that grow very fast or places that have a longer season might also have second harvest. Lastly, you may simply purposely stagger your crops harvest time.

For plants like tomatoes, they might be harvested as soon as they start blushing (showing a hint of red or pink on young green fruit). Some people prefer to let the vine ripen. If you want you might do a mixture of both so you ensure a harvest but also allow a few vine ripened tomatoes to experiment with taste. For plants like green beans there will be a period of time where the beans are all coming to size. Everyday or every few days to a couple of weeks you will be able to collect a basket of beans. For plants like lettuce, it might provide leaves all season if you cut the plant regularly and not let it go to seed.

Plants that grow on the vine can be picked by twisting them off the vine. The easier it comes off the closer to ripe the fruit is. Otherwise use a sharp pair of scissors. Don't tug or rip the piece off. Scissors provide a clean cut that is easier for the plant to heal.

EXTEND YOUR HARVEST

At the end of the season there might be some nights where it is starting to get cold. There is no long-term solution to saving your plants from the winter, but you might be able to extend their lifespan, even if it is just a little bit. One way to extend your harvest is by making sure that the plants are watered before a chilly night. This won't protect plants from frost or any foliage damage but it can keep the roots warm so the plant can thrive a little longer. This might seem like chasing the inevitable, but there are some fall days that are quite warm but the nights drop in temperature.

The other option is to cover your plants. If you have a very large garden this is not a realistic approach, but if there are a few plants that you want to give a chance to this can give them some extra room. In some cases a simple old blanket can be enough to trap some warm air, or you might use a plastic sheet to create a more efficient greenhouse effect. If you live in an area with an especially short season this might be necessary. Because of the shorter season, your plants might not be ready to harvest when the cold weather hits. By giving them just a little protection on the cooler nights you might be able to squeeze those last plants in.

AFTER THE HARVEST

Once the harvest is done you need to clean up the garden. When you do this is up to you, but your location is going to affect the window you have to do so. If you get snow soon after the first frost you need to get to work soon. If you live farther south, cleaning up one harvest might mean preparing for the next one soon after.

You need to think about how you are going to replenish the soil. Some of the plants you grew might be a good compost, some of the plants may need to be removed. You should start by removing all of the usable plant materials. Any plants that have mold or other diseases should be removed immediately.

This is a good time to go through any weeds that snuck in through the season. It is important to do this because if left alone the plant will reseed and come back twice as strong the next year. If you are using pots it's recommended that you dump out the dirt for the year and clean the pot. Unlike a bed, pots are much smaller which means the soil is likely done being useful. You might add this dirt into your compost pile.This will add some body to the compost and revitalize the soil.

If you have plants that went to seed, then get some containers and label them with each plant. Collect the seeds and store them in a cool dry place for the winter. Next year these might grow. Don't rely on them, but count them as freebies.

Pruning and Transplanting

There is debate over the best time to prune your plants. The reason there is some push not to trim your plants in the fall is twofold. The first reason is that trimming can encourage growth which is not optimal going into the winter. The second reason is that it opens up wounds on the plant that are more sensitive during the winter. In the spring the sap runs through woody plants and is more likely to heal quicker. It is better to say that pruning and trimming is not the same for every case and scenario. On the other hand if your plant is seeming weak for no identifiable reason, it is better not to cause it any more trauma.

The benefits of pruning and trimming your plants back is partly functional and partly aesthetic. When you trim your plant back you are encouraging a more appealing shape. Some plants become long and leggy without regular trimming. This makes the plant look more lush and dense. Pruning can also encourage more growth. It allows room for new growth as well, instead of putting so much energy into older growth.

If you have a dead or diseased plant it is better to cut it off when possible. Ideally if the plant has entered dormancy in the fall it is better. You don't want any issue spreading throughout the plant while it is in a weaker state like winter while you wait for spring. Plants that hold pests and mold like plants with large leaves should be cut back. Hostas for example can be a home for slug eggs. If you remove them in the fall it can cut back the population for the next year. Allowing too much organic matter to compost into the ground over winter can cause a breeding ground for disease and mold. It is good to find a balance between what to clean in the fall and what to remove in the spring, because some plants can protect the ground and beneficial bugs too.

Perennials and bushes that flower in the spring should not be cut in the fall. This is because they won't have time to regrow throughout the winter. This can end up with the plant not blooming. In this case after the plant is done flowering is the best time to prune them.

Transplanting might be necessary because of failure to thrive in one location, or maybe it was being nursed in one area and has grown strong enough or too big for its location now. Transplanting is sort of the opposite theory because it is best to transplant woody plants in the fall. This is because the increased amounts of water in the winter allows the roots to settle into their new space and become strong enough to start the new season off. Then in the next season the plant can focus on growing like usual instead of adjusting. If the plant is quite young, small. or weak it might be too hard to adjust and heal during the harsh winter. No matter what plants should not be transplanted in the summer, or even late spring. By this time the plant is starting to grow and it will not have time to adjust. In addition to the hot weather, transplanting might not just be bad for the plant but it might kill it.

For other plants, transplanting is dependent on the plant's habits. If the plant blooms in the spring, it is best to transplant in the fall, similar to trees so it has time to adjust. For plants that bloom in the fall, it is best to transplant in the spring so that you give it enough time to rest after the large amount of energy that blooming takes.

When you are transplanting, the biggest key to success is to do as little trauma as possible to the plant. The root ball of some plants might be too big to dig up, but whenever possible try to get as much root as possible. In its new location, dig the hole larger than the root ball to allow room for some new dirt on top. It is better to dig a little too deep and add more dirt, than it is to dig it too shallow. If the hole is too shallow the plant is going to have less access to soil resources and even risk falling over. Make sure to give the plant a deep drink of water to encourage root growth.

Replenish Soil Nutrients

Soil in your raised bed does not need to be completely replaced. This can be a really large project to remove the dirt, but if you are committed, every 5–10 years is more than reasonable. Instead of completely removing all of the dirt, you can add things into it to replenish it for the next season.

Mulch: Mulch is added to the soil because it helps to hold onto nutrients longer. Mulch is also especially a good idea if you are not using a raised bed, or if you have sandy soil. Sand is great for drainage but adding mulch to it in addition to other additives such as compost or manure, will allow the soil to hold on to their benefits longer. Because they are larger pieces that retain water it also prevents erosion.

PLAN FOR NEXT YEAR

Wintering

If you have perennials in your garden that are not very strong you might want to prepare them for winter by creating a shelter. For the most part the plants that you are growing in your raised bed will be annuals, but if you choose to grow plants such as lavender and you get a substantial snowfall, you might find it necessary to create a small shelter for these plants.

When it comes to covering your raised bed, it is up to you. There are benefits of covering your bed, such as preventing erosion and weeds. It can also protect any perennials. Some might be against using plastic in their raised bed and any material can risk leaving debris.

If you live in a more northern area, you are likely to face more plants completely dying off. Some plants that are self-seeding, and even plants that are supposed to be perennials, can not make it past certain temperatures. There is not a lot you can do at the end of the day, except know it isn't your fault.

Bulb Basics

Some plants grow from a bulb base like tulips, daffodils, lilies, and so on, and others like iris grow from a similar system of ribosomes. There are some debates on whether to dig them up and bring them in for the winter. In many places this is not necessary, and the bulbs and ribosomes actually benefit from the cool and wet season and in more southern areas they need to buy bulbs that have been out through a cool treatment to get them to grow. Also, a lot of these plants bloom in the early spring and there is no time to plant them before the season is over. When it might be a good idea to dig your bulbs up for the winter is if you live in a zone that is too cold for them to survive. There are tropical plants like many species of the Colocasia genus that will die. Another reason for them is an issue more specifically for ribosomes. They can start growing babies off of the mother and draining too much energy. When bulbs and ribosomes stop blooming it might mean they are getting too old and need to be replaced. For ribosomes they might benefit from being split apart and replanted.

7

CANNING AND PRESERVING

Canning and other preserving methods are not always thought about when it comes to gardening. It can seem like a whole other world, but it is a great addition to your gardening hobby. Preserving can take your gardening to another level because most people only plant what they know they can eat or give away. They aren't thinking about this food as a long-term plan. In fact many people overplant without the intention of preserving and end up wasting a lot of what they grow. Preserving can give you a little push from using gardening as a simple hobby to using it as a resource to keep food cost down because it can be used all year. Otherwise gardening for food to be eaten only fresh can be really unreliable. Plants are not always ready when you want them to be. Preserving might not be for you, but it is an option that you should explore.

WHAT IS CANNING?

When canning your food you first have to pick preservatives you are going to use, this includes vinegar, salt water, oil, or syrup/honey. The recipe for your preserved food goes beyond this of course to make it taste good, but these are the base liquids that will keep your food safe over a period of time. The second step in keeping your food safe is the sealing process. There are two canning methods: the Water-Bath and Pressure Canning. It can seem like a fairly complicated process if you haven't done it before so here is a list of things you need to know beforehand.

Once you understand the process of preserving, it seems so simple, but the most important thing to remember is that these steps are in place to keep you safe. Food that you eat from the store is full of preservatives to extend the shelf life. The food you are making has natural preservatives and the canning process to extend their life. The biggest issue with home canning is botulism which can cause food poisoning. It is very satisfying to take a step back from store made products, but to do so requires a commitment to the safety process.

Jars and Seals

The number one safety tip is to *get jars meant for canning*. Don't reuse jars if possible, especially jars from store bought products. Some products like mason jars are made with the intention of being multi-use, but if you are unsure, don't risk it. Most jarring jars are made from annealed glass, which is a treatment that makes it stronger against heat, though it is commonly mistook as tempered glass which is a type of annealed glass that has gone through a more extensive process.

Even annealed glass goes through thermal shock if warmed or cooled too quickly. The sterilization process is enough to warm the jars before adding hot products. If your jars are going to cool between these periods, make sure to heat them up again with distilled hot water. When the canning process is done, they can cool down quickly as well. In this case you may lay out a cloth on your table or counter until they cool.

Buy jars that come with lids and rings. This will ensure they are the right size. Lids that are not a perfect fit will not allow for a safe seal.

Always sterilize your jars and lids before canning anything. Your dishwasher might have a sterilized setting, otherwise you can sterilize them by hand. One method is by boiling 1:3 vinegar to water and then filling the jars. Let them sit until cool and rinse. Some might consider this method not complete enough and might submerge the jars in a pot of boiling water (possibly with vinegar) and let them boil for 10 minutes. When you've poured your contents into the jar, make sure to wipe the rim before the lid and sealing process.

The ring should be removed after canning. It can reseal a popped lid and create a contaminated false seal. If you leave it off, and the lid pops, you will be able to identify that the jar is inedible.

Always label your jars with the date, contents, and your name. This helps keep track of expiration, as well as ingredients. If you like the recipe you can make sure to follow it again. Your name is important if you are sharing with others so they can ask questions if they need to.

For convenience, consider the size of your jar. If you are planning to have a jar equal to a serving, you might adjust the jar accordingly. Also consider the opening of the jar and the food you intend to preserve. If you have large pieces like full cucumbers you might want to find a wider mouth. In addition to this, you might consider getting a funnel to help direct food into the jar.

Process

Have a clean work space with enough room to spread out while you work, canning is a messy process. When you are working with a lot of glass, it is really important to make sure you are not knocking things over. This also prevents contamination in sterilized jars.

Don't overfill your jars. If your jar is too full the contents won't have space to expand and contract with heat and can break your seal. Different recipes might call for different headspace, but leave up to an inch if you are unsure.

Work in workable batches. Sometimes recipes are not meant to be doubled. If you have two batches to do, then do two batches.

Remember that the jars are very very hot throughout the process. From the point of sterilizing, the jars will be filled with boiling food, and put in boiling water. Always take enough time in the hectic time to use safety precautions. There are jar grabbers that are made especially to have a good grip on the jars so you don't need to reach your hand close to the heat.

The jars will likely make a popping sound to indicate they are sealed. To double check it is sealed, tap the lid, if it sounds dull it has not sealed properly.

Recipe and Food

You need to add enough of your preserving agent. You should try different recipes, and follow them when you find one you like, otherwise you might not be creating a safe product. Adjusting the spices is up to you, but the amount of sugar, salt, vinegar, and water is for your safety. If you don't like the amount of one recipe, cross reference to other recipes to see if this is a necessary step.

Allow for full boil, or for the food to reach the recommended temperature, not just soft boil. Once the recipe starts to boil it can be tempting to rush the process, but the boil is not just to create a better taste and texture, but it is killing anything you don't want in your food.

Use good produce. When you are in the business of canning and processing for yourself, you might be someone who wants to prevent waste, but by adding poor ingredients into your recipe you might be creating more waste long term. Since you're cutting your food up, you can always cut blemishes and such off your food, but don't add any obviously diminished goods.

When preserving, look for preserving salt. This might also be called pickling salt and kosher salt is a close alternative.

Storing

Store your canned food in a cool, dark, dry place. If your storage space is in your basement make sure it is in a safe space that won't fall victim to seasonal flooding.

Canned food still has an expiration date. High acidity food for about a year and half, low acidity up to five years.

Use your senses. If you see there is any odd color or mold, this is not one of the products that can be just scraped off. Smell your jars when you open to make sure they smell right. Lastly, take a small taste. If you feel there is something off, don't risk it.

Water Canning vs Pressure Canning

After you are done cooking the recipe for your preserved food, you need to go through the sealing process. The two processes are water and pressure canning. Water canning is easier and much cheaper but is only effective on some foods. Pressure canning requires a pressure canner, but can be used on all preserved foods.

Water canning is only done for high acid foods, otherwise you must use a pressure cooker. It is done on the stove with a large pot. There are some pots made for this process, however any large pot will do. The most important supply is the rack that goes in the pot so the jars are not sitting directly on the heat at the bottom. The length of time to boil your jars is dependent on the size of your jars and food, starting with about 10 minutes for 4 ounce jars. The temperature of the water should be 212 °F. The water should be close to boiling when dropping the jars in so as not to cause temperature shock. For foods that you can't preserve with water canning water can, freezing is another method.

Pressure canning is done with a pressure canner device. The benefit of pressure canning is that it can preserve low acidity foods and even cooked meats. It worlds by using steam. The length and specifics will vary between devices. If you plan on using canning and preserving as a resource in your house and not just a hobby a pressure canner might be worth it to you, otherwise you might try to stick with water canning.

PICKLING RECIPE

Pickling is done with vinegar and salt to make a brine. In this brine you are able to choose the spices to adjust the flavor to your liking. While most things can be pickled, most people don't want all of their food to be pickled. The most common is of course cucumbers. The kind of cucumber you grow will make an impact on whether you have whole pickles or slices. Other common pickled food includes: onion, hot peppers (jalapeno, habanero, ect), garlic, beets, beans, radishes, and asparagus. However, if you like this method of preserving, and want to try out different foods like corn, avocado, watermelon rinds, and so on. Some people even preserve fruit this way and is used in things like salad.

Ingredients:

- 1 ⅓ cup white vinegar
- 1 cup water
- ⅓ cup sugar
- 2 tbsp salt
- Pickling food
- Spices of your choice (black and white pepper, garlic, onion, dill, cloves, star anise, and so on)

Instructions:

1. Bring brine ingredients to a boil.
2. While the brine is warming up, fill your pickling jars full with your food of choice.
3. When the brine is at a boil, bring over to your jars and pour over the food in the jars while hot.

SALT WATER

Salt water for preversing might be the most common. This is because it has the least effect on the taste of the food. Salt water brine can be used on anything from corn to lemons. Salt water canning is used in a pressure cooker almost exclusively because it does not carry the same acidity as pickling.

SALSAS AND SAUCES

Finding a salsa or sauce recipe that you like is one of my biggest recommendations when it comes to preserving and gardening. When you grow tomatoes there seems to be a million tomatoes all at once and they don't last very long. Finding a recipe where you can convert it into a sauce that you can use for the rest of the year can be a saving grace- you never want to throw out all the hard work all year. The following recipe is a tomato based sauce. If you want to make a salsa or sauce from this base you can. This is the base for preserved tomato sauce, however, adding more chunks, peppers, onions and whatever tickles your fancy is up to you.

Ingredients:

- 15 pounds tomatoes
- ¼ cup acid (vinegar or lemon juice)

Instructions:

1. Prepare a large pot of hot water on the stove and a pot of ice water.
2. Cut the stems off the tomatoes and cut a shallow X on the bottoms.
3. Drop a few tomatoes in the boiling water, after about a minute the skin will shrivel, pick it up and drop it in the ice water.
4. Continue with all of the tomatoes.
5. Drain the ice water and use your hands to peel the skin off the tomatoes.
6. Chop the tomatoes. Larger pieces mean a chunkier sauce, blend them if you want it completely smooth.
7. Add the tomatoes back into a pot and bring them to a boil.
8. Turn the heat down to a simmer and let the tomatoes reach your desired consistency which can range from half an hour to an hour and a half.

9. Add your acid and salt, stir and taste. Add more if necessary. ¼ cup is required for preserving.
10. Freeze or follow prefered canning method.

SYRUP

Fruit has a high enough acidity that it can be water canned in syrup. The syrup can be made with a 1:2 ratio of sugar to water until it thickens. The process is very similar to pickling. Prepare the fruit in warm jars and pour the hot syrup on top. Finish by water canning.

JAMS

Jam uses sugar as a way to stay preserved but instead of whole pieces they use a blended/mashed version. Jams and jellies are different from fruit suspended in syrup because they are intended to be used as a sauce or spread instead of as a whole piece. Jam can be made with less sugar and be stored in the freezer to extend its longevity. The first recipe is for freezer jams, the second is for pectin jams which is great for…

Freezer Jams

Ingredients:

- 3 pounds fruit
- 3 ½ cups sugar
- 2 tbsp lemon juice

Instructions:

1. Chop fruit into 1 inch pieces.
2. Bring to boil the fruit and sugar.
3. While heating up, continue to mash the fruit.
4. When the sugar is dissolved, add lemon juice.
5. In about 10 minutes it will bubble and fruit will float.
6. Skim foam off top.
7. Ladle into jars leaving a little room, (about an inch) at the top.
8. Put in the fridge for up to a month (freeze one year).

Pectin Jam

Ingredients:

- 5 cups fruit
- 4 cups sugar
- 1 pectin box or package
- 1 tbsp lemon juice

Instructions:

1. Combine fruit, pectin and ½ cup of sugar and bring to a boil.
2. Add the rest of the sugar and stir.
3. Bring to boil for 1 minute.
4. Remove from heat and remove foam with a spoon.
5. Ladle into jars leaving a little room at the top.
6. Add lids.
7. Add jars preferred canning method to seal.
8. Remove the ring from the lid. Otherwise the ring can create a false seal and contaminate your food.

FREEZING

However nice it is to can things, rather for quaint nostalgia or for a secure food stockpile, it might not be the option that works best for you. If you are not comfortable with canning for whatever reason, freezing is always a great method to preserve things. If you still want to make these recipes, instead of canning they can be stored in the freezer. If you want to store them as solid pieces like you might find in the grocery store that works too. Make sure to wash and dry your produce well and store them in an airtight container. Make sure to label your bag or box like you would with a jar.

DRYING HERBS

The process of drying herbs can look like a witch's house. To dry herbs, bundling them by their ends and hanging them until they are dry is the best way to preserve them for the winter. They are best when kept out of the sun. The way to improve this method is to pick apart the herbs when you are storing them. This makes them more usable. They also should be stored in jars when they are completely dry instead of simply leaving them to hang. It can be a messy job, but otherwise the herbs will lose their flavor.

PRESSING FLOWERS

Not every flower that you grow is going to be edible, but sometimes flowers are just too pretty to let die. One option to save these flowers is by pressing them. Pressing flowers is only optimal if you have a few flowers you want to preserve. Another downside is that flowers that are thicker and have a higher water content are not the best contenders for this kind of preservation. To press flowers, you just need two sheets of paper and a ton of heavy objects. Simply lay the flower flat between the pieces of paper, and stack the heavy objects on top (I always use books!). Give it a few days to a week and you should have a beautiful pressed flower!

POTPOURRI

Potpourri is a bowl of dried flowers that are treated with a scent like essential oils which is set out and used like an air freshener. Potpourri is great if you want to preserve flowers to have a use and so they retain their shape. When you are drying your flowers for potpourri you might choose to use an oven to dry them out quicker. This must be done on the lowest possible setting. You can experiment with different flowers because some flowers dry out fantastically, but some lose their color and shape.

These flowers probably won't smell like they did fresh either, that is why they should be treated with an added scent. You can put them in any kind of fancy jar that you like but a clear one will allow you to see all your pretty dried flowers. If you don't want to dry them in the oven or in the bright sunlight you might choose to hang them to dry like herbs. Some flowers will react to this better than others. Since they are hanging upside down it might change the flower's shape.

CONCLUSION

Gardening does not need to be hard. It takes time to perfect your green thumb but remember that no one is born with one, they are made. There is always going to be a margin of error for plants whether it be you or simply survival of the fittest. The goal of gardening is to figure out what works for you. It can be hard to imagine what your garden is going to look like by the end of all your hard work, but in the blink of an eye, you are going to look at your raised bed and see thick lush plants. Some plants might be dramatic and wilt after a day of imperfect conditions only to pop back up again like nothing happened, and some plants might take weeks to take a proper growth spurt. Don't get discouraged by plants that don't end up the big lush plant you imagined the first time around. It might take some tweaking to get the hang of these plant personalities.

Raised garden beds are not the only way to garden but it does provide a setting for these plants to excel from the start. Planting in the ground does work for many but raised gardening is about taking away much of this guesswork. If you've struggled in the past with getting your garden to perform at its peak then raised gardens give you a chance to garden regardless of the qualities of your soil.

Whatever flowers, vegetables, or fruit you choose to grow, it is worth the extra effort to put them in a garden that is going to thrive. Even when it comes to cost, the exponential production of plants that raise gardens provides offsets to initial cost to set up your garden bed. Instead of playing catch up every year to your garden you are able to do it right from the start. It goes to the idea of the shoe story, a poor man can only afford the cheap shoes even though they wear out every year, the rich man is able to afford shoes that last years, so he saves more in the long run. Raised gardening is the same idea, in the long run, the time it takes to set up will result in better gardening long term.

Whatever gardening that you choose to do, make a plan before you do so. Going in blind might seem fine, but you are not giving you or your garden the best chances at succeeding. Having plants with similar conditions clustered in the same place, having plants that help each other next to each other, avoiding the wrong plants. and more will result in better conditions. This plan can be helpful if you plan to can or preserve any of your harvest because you need to prepare an estimate of how much you aim to grow in supplies like jars. It is also important because you need to fit some plants in your fun too like flowers for you to enjoy.

Gardening is a hobby, a lifestyle, and a resource. It can be exciting to start and see how plants go through phases, the different ways that plants have evolved to succeed. It can give back to you. It becomes something that is necessary for your life not just in the physical sense of providing healthy food but mentally the process of growing and providing for yourself is grounding in such a busy world.

Eventually, you might not even necessarily like some of the plants you want to grow, but choose them because they are exciting to grow. It becomes interesting and a personal challenge to see what can be done in the garden. What you can tweak and turn to change the outcome of your plants. You might fall down the preserving rabbit hole, or maybe the largest pumpkin patch. You might decide to find some absurd variations of your favorite plants and food to see what the different outcomes are. The gardening world is endless and opens up a million doors to you to explore.

Despite this book being a reference to aid in your growing, there is no wrong way to have a garden. If you want to do your garden a certain way, it is best to follow what's best for the plants as best as you can, but it is your garden. As long as you stay happy and committed, you will overcome the biggest hurdle.

It all comes back to the idea that with a short list of conditions that need to be met for plants, the changes in these conditions however small make an impact. In a way we can learn from gardens to take more notice of the small details in our lives and how we can use them to improve too. A great place to start is to add more time outside in the garden enjoying the hard work and the fresh organic food for your body.

REFERENCES

A Perfect Match. (n.d.). *The Gardener*. Retrieved September 6, 2022, from https://www.thegardener.co.za/grow-to-eat/diy-food/a-perfect-match

Affeld, M. (2021, November 22). *Companion Planting For Turnips • Insteading*. Insteading. https://insteading.com/blog/companion-planting-for-turnips/

Ally. (2022, February 14). *The Best (+worst) Sweet Potato Companion Plants*. Crave the Good. https://www.cravethegood.com/sweet-potato-companion-plants/

Almanac, O. F. (n.d.). *Growing Blueberries*. Old Farmer's Almanac. https://www.almanac.com/plant/blueberries

Almanac, O. F. (n.d.-a). *Cabbage Worms*. Almanac.com. https://www.almanac.com/pest/cabbage-worms

Almanac, O. F. (2019, May 18). *Sweet Potatoes*. Old Farmer's Almanac. https://www.almanac.com/plant/sweet-potatoes

Beaulieu, D. (2021, August 25). *11 Types of Mint Plants for Your Garden*. The Spruce. https://www.thespruce.com/types-of-mint-5120608

Bonvissuto, D. (n.d.). *Kale Yes! One Leafy Green's Many Merits*. HGTV. https://www.hgtv.com/outdoors/flowers-and-plants/kale-yes-one-leafy-greens-many-merits

Clark, J. (n.d.). *Common Arugula Varieties - Learn about Different Types of Arugula*. Https://Www.tipsbulletin.com. https://www.tipsbulletin.com/types-of-arugula/

Crow, R. (2022, July 1). *Tomato companion planting – what to grow alongside tomatoes for a great crop*. Homesandgardens.com. https://www.homesandgardens.com/advice/tomato-companion-planting

Dyer, M. (2022, May 25). *Borage Varieties*. Www.gardeningknowhow.com. https://www.gardeningknowhow.com/edible/herbs/borage/different-borage-flowers.htm

Essential Nutrients for Plants. (2021, December 7). Texas A&M Agrilife

Extension Service. https://agrilifeextension.tamu.edu/asset-exter nal/essential-nutrients-for-plants/

Fillmore Container. (2021, April 1). *Are Canning Jars Tempered?* Fillmore Container. https://www.fillmorecontainer.com/blog/2021/04/01/are-canning-jars-tempered-fillmore-container-get-the-facts-on-tempering-vs-annealing/

Flint, M. L. (2011). Whiteflies Management Guidelines. Uc IMP. http://ipm.ucanr.edu/PMG/PESTNOTES/pn7401.html

Gavin, J. (2019, June 5). *Types of Broccoli.* Jessica Gavin. https://www.jessicagavin.com/types-of-broccoli/

Grant, A. (2021, May 15). *Eggplant Seed Preparation: Tips For Growing Eggplant Seeds.* Www.gardeningknowhow.com. https://www.gardeningknowhow.com/edible/vegetables/eggplant/growing-eggplant-seeds.htm

Grant, A. (2021b, June 18). *Rosemary Plant Types: Varieties Of Rosemary Plants For The Garden.* Www.gardeningknowhow.com. https://www.gardeningknowhow.com/edible/herbs/rosemary/rosemary-plant-varieties.htm

Grant, A. (2022a, July 25). *Kale Companion Plants: Learn About Plants That Grow Well With Kale.* Www.gardeningknowhow.com. https://www.gardeningknowhow.com/edible/vegetables/kale/kale-companion-plants.htm

Grant, A. (2022, July 27). *Companion Plants For Chard: What Grows Well With Chard.* Www.gardeningknowhow.com. https://www.gardeningknowhow.com/edible/vegetables/swiss-chard/chard-companion-plants.htm

Greenleaf, J. (2020, August 21). *How to Get Rid of Moles Using Home Remedies.* MYMOVE. https://www.mymove.com/pest-control/remove-moles/

H, J. (2022, February 21). *14 Varieties of Thyme: Choose Your Favorite Type For The Garden.* The Culinary Herb Garden. https://howtoculinaryherbgarden.com/varieties-of-thyme/

Hailey, L. (2021, November 22). *Swiss Chard Varieties: 12 Types of Chard Cultivars You'll Love.* All about Gardening. https://www.allaboutgardening.com/swiss-chard-varieties/

Homestratosphere's Editorial Staff & Writers. (2020, August 12). *13 Different Types of Celery – Who Knew, Right?* Home Stratosphere. https://www.homestratosphere.com/types-of-celery/

How to Build a Raised Garden Bed. (n.d.). The Home Depot. https://www.homedepot.com/c/ah/how-to-build-raised-garden-beds/9ba683603be9fa5395fab90b41bb0da

How to Grow Sweet Corn from Seed | Guides. (n.d.). OSC Seeds. https://www.oscseeds.com/resources/how-to-grow-guides/how-to-grow-corn-from-seed/

Lamp'l, J. (2018, March 8). Raised Bed Garden. Joe Gardener® | Organic Gardening like a Pro. https://joegardener.com/podcast/raised-bed-gardening-pt-1/

List of tomato cultivars. (2022, April 8). Wikipedia. https://en.wikipedia.org/wiki/List_of_tomato_cultivars

Macdonald, M. (2021, April 6). *How to Grow Cucumbers.* West Coast Seeds. https://www.westcoastseeds.com/blogs/how-to-grow/grow-cucumbers

Malkin, N. (2021, April 16). *Can Epsom Salt Help in the Garden?* This Old House. https://www.thisoldhouse.com/gardening/22386000/epsom-salt-in-garden

Martens Forney, J. (n.d.). *What to Prune in Late Fall.* HGTV. https://www.hgtv.com/outdoors/gardens/planting-and-maintenance/what-to-prune-in-late-fall

MasterClass. (2021a, June 7). *Lettuce Companion Planting.* MasterClass. https://www.masterclass.com/articles/lettuce-companion-planting-guide

MasterClass. (2021b, June 21). *Potato Companion Planting.* MasterClass. https://www.masterclass.com/articles/potato-companion-planting-guide

Michaels, K. (2009). *Don't Make These Common Seed Starting Mistakes.* The Spruce. https://www.thespruce.com/growing-seeds-indoors-common-mistakes-847800

Moulton, A. M. (2021, August 23). *12 Rose Companion Plants (& What Not To Grow Near Roses).* Blooming Backyard. https://www.bloomingbackyard.com/rose-companion-plants/

REFERENCES

Nolan, T. (2021, September 27). *Garlic Varieties: Choosing the Types of Garlic to Grow in Your Garden.* Savvy Gardening. https://savvygardening.com/garlic-varieties/

Painter, T. (2020, April 19). *Turnip Varieties.* Home Guides | SF Gate. https://homeguides.sfgate.com/turnip-varieties-22267.html

Potato Types | Different Types of Potatoes | Potato Goodness. (n.d.). Potatoes USA. https://potatogoodness.com/potato-types/

Regina. (2022, January 12). *Fennel: varieties, growing, propagation & care.* Plantura. https://plantura.garden/uk/vegetables/fennel/fennel-overview

Richard. (2018, April 16). *What Is The Best Fertilizer For Growing Potatoes?* GrowerExperts.com. https://www.growerexperts.com/what-is-the-best-fertilizer-for-growing-potatoes/

Sow True Seed. (n.d.). *The Different Types of Carrots, Explained for Home Gardeners.* Sow True Seed. https://sowtrueseed.com/blogs/gardening/types-of-carrots

Spengler, T. (2022, May 26). *Companion Planting With Celery: What Are Some Good Celery Companion Plants.* Www.gardeningknowhow.com. https://www.gardeningknowhow.com/edible/vegetables/celery/celery-companion-plants.htm

Spengler, T. (2022b, July 10). *Best Times For Transplanting: When Is A Good Time To Transplant In The Garden.* Www.gardeningknowhow.com. https://www.gardeningknowhow.com/ornamental/shrubs/shgen/best-times-for-transplanting.htm

Sweetser, R. (2022, June 15). *Canning for Beginners: What Is Canning?* Old Farmer's Almanac. https://www.almanac.com/canning-for-beginners

Thornbro, H. (2021, July 14). *What NOT To Plant Near Blueberries.* Redemption Permaculture. https://redemptionpermaculture.com/what-not-to-plant-near-blueberries/

Turnips & Rutabagas – Produce Blue Book. (n.d.). Blue Book Services. https://www.producebluebook.com/know-your-commodity/turnips-rutabagas/

Types of Lettuce. (n.d.). The Home Depot. https://www.homedepot.com/c/ab/types-of-lettuce/9ba683603be9fa5395fab9090a446f7

Van Druff, K. (2021, October). *Lavender Companion Plants: Vegetables, Flowers & Herbs*. Bunny's Garden. https://www.bunnysgarden.com/lavender-companion-plants/

Ware, M. (2017, May 19). *Swiss chard: Possible health benefits, uses, and risks*. Www.medicalnewstoday.com. https://www.medicalnewstoday.com/articles/284103#potential_health_risks

Watson, M. (2019). *Learn the Different Types of Cucumbers and How to Use Them*. The Spruce Eats. https://www.thespruceeats.com/cucumber-varieties-4069657

What are the Different Types of Spinach? (2017, May 26). Gardening Ideas, Tips, Trends and Information - Ugaoo.com Blog. https://www.ugaoo.com/knowledge-center/types-of-spinach-or-spinach-varieties/

White, J. (2021, August 22). *Asparagus Types: 15 Asparagus Varieties To Grow in Your Garden*. All about Gardening. https://www.allaboutgardening.com/asparagus-types

Printed in Great Britain
by Amazon